Standard-Bred Orpington Chickens
Chicken Breeds Book 11

by J.H. Drevenstedt

with an introduction by Jackson Chambers

This work contains material that was originally published in 1911.

This publication is within the Public Domain.

Introduction

I am pleased to present this eleventh title in the "Chicken Breeds" series.

This volume is entitled "Standard Bred Orpingtons" and was authored by J.H. Drevenstedt in 1910.

The work is in the Public Domain and is re-printed here in accordance with Federal Laws.

Though this work is a century old, "The Orpingtons" contains much information on this well known chicken breed that is still pertinent today.

Jackson Chambers
Josephine County, Oregon

Kellerstrass Farm

Arthur Oscar Schilling
1907

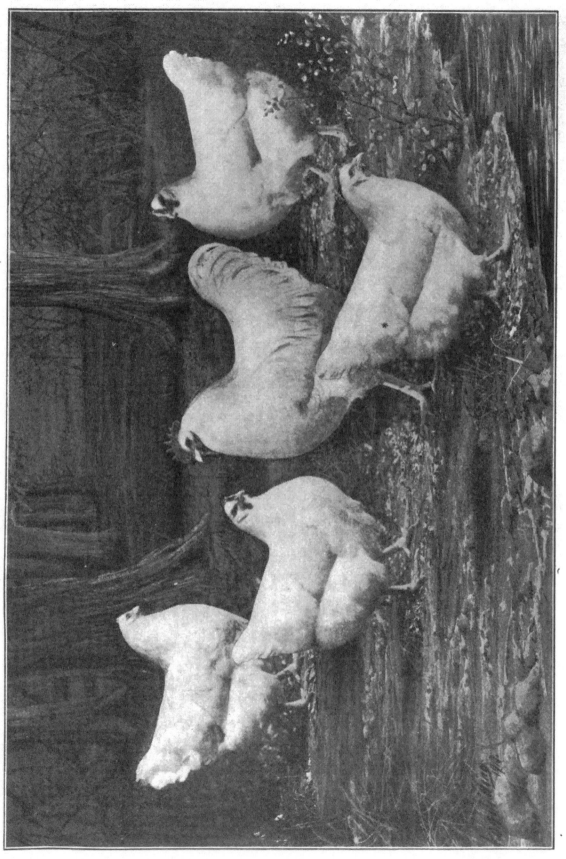

The Orpingtons

Table of Contents

INTRODUCTORY

THIS BREED BOOK, devoted to the Orpington race of domesticated poultry, is the first and most complete of its kind published in America. England has produced many Standard-bred varieties of superior merit and surpassing beauty in the past, but we have no hesitation in stating that its newest production, the Orpington, is the most universally popular breed ever originated in Great Britain. Not only in England, but in Australia, Canada, and the United States as well, are Orpingtons enjoying unbounded popularity. The intrinsic merit of the Orpington fowl for utilitarian purposes, its commanding size and solid type, combined with beauty of plumage, are invaluable assets that assure its permanent popularity.

That a book giving an authentic history of the origin of the Orpington, its development as a Standard-bred fowl, its value as a layer and meat producer, and a description of its fine exhibition points, with proper illustrations for mating, breeding and judging all varieties of Orpingtons, is needed, is obvious.

In undertaking the task of compiling a book of this character, I did it with a feeling of a responsibility greater perhaps than the results may show, but readers can rest assured that a careful research has been made into the history of the breed from its origin to its final development into three Standard and eight non-Standard varieties. For most of the important data relating to the above I am indebted to the Lewis Wright's "Book of Poultry," E. Campbell's book, "The Orpington And Its Varieties," both standard English works; also to letters and articles written by the originator, William Cook, Captain Gedney, Harrison Weir, Wallace P. Willett, and others.

To the Reliable Poultry Journal, American Poultry World, D. E. Hale, A. O. Schilling, and many prominent American breeders of Orpingtons grateful acknowledgment is due for their valuable contributions to the different chapters of this book. Special attention is directed to the beautiful illustrations by Franklane L. Sewell, Arthur O. Schilling and I. W. Burgess. This art work is one of the great features of this book, unrivalled and unapproachable in beauty of design and finish.

Having made a study of the Orpington fowl as a judge at the earlier exhibits held at Madison Square Garden Shows, New York, and at other large shows in the East, South and Canada up to the present day, the task has been a congenial one and the conclusions arrived at are the result of an impartial judgment of the facts as they appeared to me. That "The Orpingtons" will prove a valuable aid to breeders of one of the most popular breeds in the world is the sincere wish of the undersigned.

J. H. DREVENSTEDT.

New York, 1910.

THE FAMOUS PEN OF WHITE ORPINGTONS SOLD FOR $7,500.00 TO MADAME PADEREWSKI
BY THE KELLERSTRASS FARM.

CHAPTER I

Orpington Origin

Authentic History of the Origin of Black, White, Buff, Spangled and Jubilee Orpingtons—Black Orpington
First Produced and Exhibited in America in 1890—Claims of Other Originators in Producing Buff
and White Orpingtons—History of the Different English Strains of the Three Standard
and the Eight Non-Standard Varieties of Orpingtons

J. H. Drevenstedt

TWENTY years ago Orpingtons were exhibited in America for the first time, the Single Comb Black Orpington being the original variety shown. It was the first of a distinctly new breed of fowl originated in 1886 by William Cook of Orpington, County of Kent, England, whence Orpingtons take their name. Being "English, you know," it took American poultry breeders some years to become interested and enthusiastic over Orpingtons. Objections to fowls with black legs and white skin were lodged against Black Orpingtons and later the white or pink legs and white skin of Buff and White Orpingtons was considered a serious market handicap, as American markets demanded yellow-skinned and yellow-legged poultry. So the doom of the Orpingtons was predicted before breeders on this side of the Atlantic became acquainted with the good qualities of this new English race of fowl, or realized that a master hand at promoting and advertising new breeds was at work in England, Australia and America, boosting the breed he originated, by lavish use of printer's ink which included much free advertising for himself—for the originator was a clever writer on poultry topics, as well as a very shrewd breeder and dealer. The superior qualities of his Orpingtons were "laid on with a thick brush," the defects he kept in the background. The result of all these persistent and insistent claims of superiority over all other breeds is that Orpingtons are today the most popular fowl in England and have made such rapid strides toward popularity in this country, notably in White Orpingtons, that they have become dangerous rivals of the American Plymouth Rocks, Wyandottes, Rhode Island Reds and Leghorns. The originator,

William Cook, died in 1904, at a time when Orpingtons were beginning to boom rapidly, thanks to the late and lamented Mr. Cook and the hustling and able efforts of Wallace P. Willett of East Orange, N. J., editor and publisher of "The Orpington." This was before the day of Owen Farms, Ernest Kellerstrass and other "big guns" of the Orpington fancy of today, Charles Vass, Dr. Paul Kyle, Wallace P. Willett, Frank W. Gaylor and William Davis being the pioneers in the early Buff Orpington days; but when Mr. Cook appeared at the Madison Square Garden, New York, in 1903 with a great string of English Orpingtons and received fulsome press notices in the daily papers of his exhibits, arranged in a clever manner at one end of the big show arena, the real Orpington boom in the United States and Canada was launched. As an advance agent, William Cook was in a class by himself; as a salesman he was a star, the prices realized by him for Orpingtons at that memorable show being exceedingly high. The purchasers were men of wealth, as a rule, who realized that aside from the fancy end, it would be a good business investment as well. A study of the comparative growth in popularity of Orpingtons in D. E. Hale's article on another page of this book, will justify the judgment of these shrewd fanciers who bought at that time.

THE LATE WM. COOK,
Originator of the Orpington Fowl

Orpingtons First Exhibited in America in 1890

Single Comb Black Orpingtons were first exhibited at the show of the Massachusetts Poultry Association, held in Boston in 1890. Single Comb Buff Orpingtons were first exhibited at the Madison Square Garden Show, New York, in 1899, twelve single entries and one pen being the total. In 1901 the entries increased to nineteen single and

FIRST PRIZE PEN S·C· WHITE ORPINGTONS AT PITTSBURGH 1910.
BRED AND OWNED BY
LAWRENCE JACKSON   HAYSVILLE PA.

one pen of Buff Orpingtons, Charles Vass, Wallace P. Willett and Doctor Paul Kyle being the exhibitors. At New York in 1909-10 157 Single Comb Buff, 122 Single Comb Black, 134 Single Comb White, 17 Diamond Jubilee, 5 Spangled, 25 Rose Comb Buff, 13 Rose Comb Black and 5 Rose Comb White Orpingtons were exhibited, making a total of 478 Orpingtons—a remarkable showing for a breed of English origin in a country where there was supposed to be little demand for poultry with white skin and white or black shanks.

Early Orpington History

Wallace P. Willett of East Orange, New Jersey, sends us the following interesting data relating to the early history of the Orpingtons:

"I have been keeping fancy fowls as a hobby not as a business, except in certain instances, for the past fifty years, and have handled in that time almost every nameable breed from the Shanghai, my first purchase in the eighteen fifties, up to the present time. I was always on the lookout for something new and promising in the poultry world—at home and abroad. When the Anconas started to boom in England I brought them here and trap-nested them for four years or more, but gave them up as not filling the bill for an all round purpose fowl.

"The October, 1897, number of Farm Poultry printed a picture of Wm. Cook and of his Black and Buff Orpingtons and the editorial correspondence of A. F. Hunter, who was then visiting poultry plants in England, gave an interesting account of meeting Mr. Cook, who personally showed him about his poultry farm near Orpington village. Mr. Hunter said that Mr. Cook's business included the shipment of 10,404 sittings of eggs in nine months. This and more written by Editor Hunter gave me the Orpington fever at once and I immediately entered into correspondence which resulted in one importation early in 1898 of Black, Buff and White Orpington eggs, direct from Mr. Cook's farm, from which my first Orpington chicks of these varieties were hatched. I made a second importation by steamer in September of the same year. Up to that year, 1898, no Buff or White Orpingtons had been brought into the United States, but perhaps a dozen Blacks had come in.

"Daniel Love exhibited a Black cock and two hens at Worcester, Mass., in January, 1891, and Wm. McNeil, London, Canada, entered one Black cockerel at the Boston show, in 1897. Four Blacks were exhibited at New York, in 1896 by C. S. Williams, New Jersey, and five Blacks were shown at New York, in 1898, by Geo. M. Shaw.

"A careful examination of poultry records shows no other entries at poultry exhibitions in the United States. The few Black Orpingtons exhibited had not caused the breed to make much progress here.

"In 1898 C. E. Vass, Washington, N. J., brought over a pen of Buff Orpingtons from "a successful breeder in England," not from Wm. Cook direct, and exhibited them at Mount Gretna, Pa. This was the first exhibit of Buff Orpingtons in America.

"In September, 1898, R. S. Templin, Colla, Ohio, advertised 'A few Buff Orpington pullets wanted in exchange for one or two cockerels.'

"In 1899 Mr. Vass made two entries at Boston and he and his neighbors made seventeen entries at New York. At Philadelphia in 1899, there were two exhibited and this is the record of Buffs up to January, 1900.

"The exhibits of 1899 served to call attention to their merits and there was quite a little demand for Orpington eggs. At the New York show, in 1900, there were some 43

entries. The writer made his first exhibit at this show, entering two Blacks and two Buffs, winning two firsts on Blacks but nothing on Buffs. The 'Cook Type' of Buffs had not been judged before and differed somewhat from the 'Vass Type' which had already been judged. It was the only type known previous to the showing of the 'Cook Orpingtons' but the latter came to the front immediately after."

William Cook's Story of the Origin.

In 1890 Mr. Cook contributed several articles to the English poultry press, which purport to give the true origin of the Black Orpington—the pioneer of this new breed—at the same time setting forth in bold relief the claims of its being the possessor of the finest flesh and skin in existence. As a matter of history we give William Cook's own story of his object in creating the Orpington fowl, as follows:

"I have heard it said by some persons when going around a big poultry show that there are so many useful varieties, it is difficult to decide which breed of fowls to go in for. It certainly is puzzling to an amateur, and even those who have kept fowls for years, when they make a change in their breed are somewhat in a fix as to which is the best for them to go in for. Those who have kept a breed successfully for years are loud in their praises, and say they are the best breed which can possibly be kept (and very often they have not kept any other breed at all). It is usually the amateur poultry keepers who are so enthusiastic over their results. Unfortunately many practical men and women will not take the trouble to place their poultry results on record, by writing to say how they have obtained such results, etc. I have heard some say: 'If we tell others of our success and mode of working they will be as wise as ourselves.' Since poultry papers have become so popular the truth of the old adage, 'Giving does not impoverish,' has been proved. There is a class of people who say that we have enough breeds of poultry as it is, without making any fresh ones. The Americans, however, have not paid any heed to murmurings, but have kept pace with the times, and have brought out some breeds of poultry which have been much appreciated, not only in America, but throughout the world, and perhaps more in this England of ours than in any other part of the globe. The Plymouth Rock originated in America, and no breed has held such a reputation as a useful fowl all through England as the Plymouth Rock. The Americans saw that they went well, and they soon had another for us, viz., the Wyandotte. This breed has taken fairly well, and has been much improved since its arrival in England; but what the Americans believe to be perfection the English object to. They think that a good yellow skin is the best for table fowls to possess, whereas English customers like to see a nice white skin on fowls, especially when they have to go through the markets.

"I may mention here that I have had many years' experience in crossing fowls, and I have tried as many as fifty crosses in a year, for the purpose of testing which cross is the most suited to various circumstances. I used to have birds at different parts of the country, so as to enable me to try experiments with the various breeds and their crosses, and this I did for many years, but had not at that time the least idea of publishing the result. The idea did not enter my head until after I had had twenty years of experience in this line. I commenced very young. To try so many crosses I had, of course, to use pure varieties of almost every breed, and in doing so I had a fair opportunity to judge which were the best pure breeds. I have found good layers of every breed, and I have never yet kept any breed of fowls some of which did not lay all through the winter months. In this way I proved that the laying powers of the fowls are not so much regulated by the breed as by the strain. I found that the Plymouth Rock stood at the head of the list, for laying and table qualities combined, for some years, but an idea occurred to me that I could improve even on this. I will mention (1) how I did it, and (2) why. I believed that a better all round fowl could be produced for laying and table purposes, which would at the same time suit the public. I found out, by visiting many exhibitions and poultry yards, that some liked the Minorca fowls, but that their white-shelled eggs and big combs, which so soon get frost-

BLACK ORPINGTON COCKEREL—ENGLISH-AMERICAN
TYPE

Picture shows first prize Black Orpington cockerel at Madison Square Garden, December, 1908-January, 1909, as exhibited by Wm. Cook & Sons, Kent, England and Scotch Plains, New Jersey, U. S. A. The Cook Farm at Scotch Plains is in charge of Percy A. Cook, eldest son of the late Wm. Cook, principal originator and early promoter of all varieties of the Orpington fowls.

bitten, were drawbacks to them. Then others fancied the Langshan, but did not like the feathers on their legs. Some had a fancy for the Black Rocks, but as they were only sports from the speckled, and not an established breed, they did not take as they otherwise would have done. I took this all in, and resolved that from these three useful breeds I could and would produce a bird to suit the public. I took the three breeds, and commenced mating Minorca cocks with Black Rock hens, then Langshan cocks to the above hens. I may mention that I used birds which exhibitors would have termed 'useless'— Minorca cockerels with red in their ear-lobes, which caused them to be unsuitable for breeding pure birds; the black

Plymouth Rock hens thrown on one side by exhibitors as being sports only from the grey; and the clean-legged Langshans of no use whatever to breed birds such as were required by the standard of the Langshan Club at that time. Such birds as these were put on one side for laying purposes or for the pot.

"Now, it is generally admitted by the breeders of all these varieties (Langshans, Minorcas and Plymouth Rocks) that the birds which I selected—the so-called 'useless' ones—are the best layers of their kind. Take Minorcas, for instance, which have red or otherwise bad ear lobes. They are usually the finest birds and lay before their more perfect sisters. Black Rocks frequently lay a month or six weeks before the speckled birds and they grow into the finest shaped birds also.

"Langshans that come clean on the leg are also the best layers. When I began to breed I started with four pens of birds so that I might have unrelated strains to avoid in-breeding, and then I only kept those which were the type which I had in my mind's eye. It is only by careful selection that a good bird or animal can be produced. This breed has been before the public for three and a half years, and they have made such rapid strides that they have increased and spread over the country with wonderful rapidity. Wherever a pen of birds or setting of eggs go, more are sent for. They are capital winter and summer layers and very hardy, as they stand the wet and cold climates well. I have found them the best winter layers of brown eggs that I have ever kept, and hundreds of other breeders say the same. At the same time they are very handsome fowls. The first year they were out I only exhibited two birds at Crystal Palace, two at the Dairy Show and two at Birmingham, and I received orders for them from all parts of England. I was not prepared for these orders and could not supply them. I only had about sixty stock birds on hand and could not spare any of these until after I had done breeding.

"I sold about two hundred sittings of eggs from them the first year. Classes were provided for them in 1887, and they were acknowledged as a pure breed. The leading shows provided classes for them in 1888, including Crystal Palace, Dairy and Windsor shows and others. I may mention that in 1887 a club was formed, which did a good work in providing specials, etc., at the various shows for the further development of the breed. Of course, this interested secretaries in the variety and induced them to provide classes.

"The Orpingtons have the finest flesh and skin of any fowl in existence, unless it is the Langshan, and they develop more quickly than do the Langshans or Plymouth Rocks; and if chickens of the three kinds are reared together, it will be found that the Orpingtons will generally grow right away from the others. I have seen cockerels turn the scale at nine, nine and a half and ten pounds at six months old. They are spoken of by those who have tried them as the best of table fowls. Of course they have black legs, which is against them in the London markets, but after a person has once dined off one he puts up with the black legs for the sake of the delicious meat, which is much the same as a young turkey's in flavor and color. As regards the eating part, I am sure no breed can surpass them. As I have said, they are splendid table fowls, good winter layers of brown eggs, and very handsome in the bargain. My pens are always open for inspection six days in the week.

"The Orpingtons have single combs, standing erect in the cocks, and the hen's may either stand up or fall over to one side; red face and ear-lobes, black beak, very broad breast and long breast bone; flesh white, plumage black throughout, with a splendid green sheen. The cocks have long tails, with very fine hangers (feathers at the side of the tail.) They have a number of these feathers which give the birds a very graceful appearance. The tail should be carried well back, not straight up; the legs are black, and free from any tint of yellow, a little red, however, not being objectionable; four toes on each foot. The feet should be white underneath. The hens should in every way correspond with the male bird, except that the comb should be smaller. If it is evenly serrated and straight, it may fall a little to one side. The tail, of course, is smaller."

Origin of the Rose Comb Black Orpington

Of the Rose Comb Black Orpingtons, also originated by Mr. Cook, the latter writes, in the same year:

"Lately another variety has been introduced; namely, the Rose Comb Orpington. This is a breed which stands right away from all the rest, and there is no other large breed of black rose combs in England. The Black Hamburgs are small birds, with white ear lobes, and lay white eggs, whereas the Rose Comb Orpingtons lay brown eggs. I am often asked which of the two varieties—the Orpington and the Rose Comb Orpington—is the better to keep. My answer is, that it is more a matter of fancy, as they differ very slightly in regard to their useful qualities. The Rose Comb Orpingtons lay rather the more eggs, but they are not so large in size as the Orpingtons. The weight of eggs produced in a year does not vary, the quality of the flesh is equal, and also the fowls' appearance, except that they differ in the matter of their combs. Many people, I

ROSE COMB BLACK ORPINGTON COCK, 1890.

find, have an idea that the rose comb variety have Black Hamburg blood in them, but this is altogether a mistake.

"About fifteen years ago there were some Langshans imported into England with rose combs. They were mated with Langshans with the orthodox single comb, but many

of the progeny came with rose combs. No notice was taken of this, and many were killed and eaten. Fortunately I got hold of a few, and bred from them, and I bought as many as I could about the country, until I had a nice flock together. Then I crossed them in the same manner as I

ROSE COMB BLACK ORPINGTON HEN, 1890.

had done to get the single comb variety, using the Rose Comb Langshan instead of the others. I wish my readers to understand that the rose comb is obtained by a freak of nature, and not from any existing breed of fowls. These freaks of nature are called 'sports.'

All poultry keepers who have had experience in breeding rose comb breeds of fowls know that they do not all come with rose combs, although their parents all possessed rose combs. The Rose Comb Orpington is not an exception to this rule, and being a newly-made breed, it can scarcely be expected, when an old established breed like the Black Hamburg throws birds with single combs. Of the cockerels also, a few come slightly mismarked with red feathers, instead of being black throughout, as they should be. Some people think it strange that the cockerel should be thus marked, but it is a frequent occurrence that when two black breeds are mated together, their progeny will throw red feathers in their hackles and saddles.

"The Rose Comb Orpington cock should be black throughout, with a splendid green gloss upon the plumage, broad in the breast, and with a nice flowing tail, carried well back, black beak well curved, dark or hazel eyes, the former preferred, and a neat rose comb, closely fitted to the head, with a short spike at the back, red face and ear-lobes, black legs with white toe nails, four toes on each foot; the sole of the foot being white. The hen should match the male bird in all points, only the comb and tail are smaller. The chickens are very hardy and can be brought up in small runs and often lay at six months old.

No one who has tried them is disappointed with them, as they fill the egg basket when the snow is on the ground."

The Rose Comb Black Orpington cock and hen illustrated on page 9 are reprints from the "Fancier's Gazette," England, 1890, and represent the Ideal Orpington of that time. As might be expected, there was much adverse criticism at that time over these newcomers in the poultry field, not only in England but in America. Our own comments on Mr. Cook's article were published in the Fancier's Journal, Philadelphia, Pa., July 19th, 1890, which read in part as follows:

"Our information regarding this breed comes from a gentleman who visited the yards of the originator in England for the express purpose of buying Orpingtons. He was thoroughly disappointed in the latter, and stated to us that there was nothing uniform about the look of the birds.

"In reading Mr. Cook's article one can plainly see the attempt to push these birds ahead of all other breeds. It is a transparent dodge to catch the usual dollar. They are so immensely superior to other varieties that about the only thing we can do is to invest at once and buy a few. The Black Java is one of the best fowls we have, and the Single Comb Orpington could scarcely be men-

WINNER OF FIRST PRIZE, NEW YORK, DEC. 1907.
BRED AND OWNED BY OWEN FARMS, VINEYARD HAVEN, MASS.

BUFF ORPINGTON PULLET—AMERICAN
TYPE

tioned in the same breath with that thoroughbred fowl. The assertion that the Rose Comb Orpington fills a place of its own is erroneous, as we have a black Wyandotte in this country which will fully equal the Orpington in useful qualities and surpass it in breeding qualities. The Black Wyandotte is a true sport—not a cross.

"In bolstering up the excessive good qualities of the Orpington the originator makes some very queer state-

ments. He says: 'Take Minorcas, for instance, which have red or otherwise bad ear-lobes. They are usually the finest birds and lay before their more perfect sisters.' This will surprise many breeders who pin their faith on white ear-lobed birds as layers. The great records made by Hamburgs, Leghorns and Andalusians as egg-producers would, according to the above statement, be vastly improved if the white ear-lobes were bred out. He goes on to say: 'Black Rocks frequently lay a month or six weeks before the speckled birds, and they grow into the finest shaped birds also.' This is another surprise. Close observer, that Mr. Cook, but Plymouth Rock breeders will smile at the assertion. It reminds me of the statement made by a friend who bought some White Rocks. He claimed that they laid 'way head of the Barred,' but subsequently found out that he was breeding a cross-bred Leghorn-Brahma instead of a White Rock.

"The most radical statement made is that 'Langshans that come clean on the leg are also the best layers.' Anything to boom the clean-legged, black, red ear-lobed Orpington will answer the fertile-brained originator. The feathers on the legs of birds have nothing to do with laying eggs. If so we had better discard all feather-legged breeds."

The above was written twenty years ago when we had the Missouri habit, "wanting to be shown," as well as having a membership in the Doubting Thomas Club. The world, especially the poultry world, moves rapidly, the scenery changing suddenly in unexpected places, so we must take off our hat to the Orpington fowl today and accord to William Cook the honor of having built not better than he knew, but what he knew in the beginning would prove a new and popular breed of poultry.

Origin of Other Varieties of Orpingtons

Although the general belief is that William Cook originated not only the Black Orpington, but also the Whites, Buffs, Jubilee and Spangled varieties, there are English authorities on poultry who dispute Mr. Cook's claim as the originator of the Buff and White varieties, but accord him the sole credit of producing the Blacks, Jubilee and Spangles. Mr. Cook as far back as 1880, before the Black Orpingtons made their appearance, was busy crossing White Leghorn cocks with Black Hamburg pullets, and mating the white pullets from this cross with White Dorking cocks; but it took him nearly ten years to get a perfect white fowl and eliminate the fifth toe of the Dorking, specimens of which he exhibited in 1889.

In order to get the true facts regarding the origin of all the varieties of Orpingtons, D. E. Hale, Associate Editor of the Reliable Poultry Journal, made a careful study of the English poultry press and books and prepared a special article on the subject for this book. Excepting Black Orpingtons, which are described by the originator in the preceding pages, the origin of all other varieties is clearly stated by Mr. Hale as follows:

The Buff Orpington

There has always been considerable dispute as to how the Buffs were originated. Mr. Cook claimed he produced them by making the following crosses: He first crossed Golden Spangled Hamburgs with Buff Cochins. The offspring he crossed with dark or colored Dorkings; the progeny of this cross were bred back to Buff Cochins and produced the Buff Orpington. The following diagram will perhaps give a clearer idea of how the crosses were made:

Buff Orp.	Hamb. Coch. Dork. Ck.	Dark Dork. Ck.	Gold. Ham. Ck.
	Buff Cochin Hens	Ham. Coch. P'l'ts	Bf. Coch. Fem'l

There had been in existence for a long time a fowl that was raised mostly in the county of Lincoln and was known as Lincolnshire Buffs. Mr. E. Brown says as follows:

"Birds of a similar type have been personally known to us for more than twenty years, especially in the Spalding, Boston and Louth districts, under the name of Lincolnshire Buff. They were, however, more of the Cochin type, due to want of definite aim in breeding and careful selection, but were, as a rule, white skinned and legged, and the great majority had feathers down the leg. Hence, what Mr. Cook states he had accomplished by specific matings, was already in existence, only needing the attention of breeders to secure uniformity and refinement of type.

"Lincolnshire breeders regard the breed as having been formed thus:

Lincolnshire Buff	Buff Cochin Male		
	Dorking—Common Cross	Dorking	
		Common Fowl	

"Even if we accept the statement that some of the Buff Orpingtons were produced in Kent, there is an abundance of evidence that the great majority of many present-day Buffs are directly bred from Lincolnshire Buffs, without the slightest relationship to Mr. Cook's strain; or, as Mr. R. de Courcy Peele, in his book, 'Orpingtons and All About Them,' says: 'The foundation had been laid many years previous to Mr. Cook's time in the shape of the Lincolnshire Buff, a variety, if it may be so called, which has for many years been the acknowledged farmer's fowl in and about Spalding and the neighboring towns.'"

Owing to the controversy which was carried on in England for some time, relative to the origin and name given the Buffs by Mr. Cook, and as we have never seen the matter explained in print in this country, we again quote from Mr. Brown's Book, "Domestic Races of Fowls," in order to give the American fanciers both sides of the question. We have heard how Mr. Cook originated his Buffs; now let us see what others said about it.

"Around the Buffs a fierce contest arose, not in respect to the qualities or the characteristics of the variety, but the name. It is not our purpose to go over this ground, as the doing so would be futile. Apart from all questions as to the claims put regarding the origin, as to whether—which is our belief—the Buff Orpington is a refined Lincolnshire Buff, as to whether Mr. Cook did not buy Lincolnshire Buffs before he introduced Buff Orpingtons, as to whether he did not sell Lincolnshire Buffs as Buff Orpingtons, and as to whether birds identical and bred from the same parents have not been, and are still sold under both designations, there is an important question as to name.

"When Mr. Cook brought out the breed in 1894 the Orpington Club protested strongly against the use of the name Orpington, and others did the same. The question was ably summed up by Mr. Lewis Wright in his book entitled 'The New Book of Poultry,' as follows: 'A breeder might justifiably use any name he likes really open to him; but when a man has already appropriated the name of his residence to one breed, of which he tells us the components were A. B. and C, there are the gravest objections to his giving, years afterwards, the same name for merely trade and advertising purposes, to another breed which, according to his own account, has no particle of A, B, and C, but was built up of X, Y, Z.'

"With these observations we absolutely agree, and the Poultry Club failed lamentably in recognizing the name under these conditions.

"The thing is done, and cannot now be altered. The 'canniness' which designed the coup has had its reward. But we feel that a grave injustice has been done to Lincolnshire breeders. The advertising they would have reaped has gone elsewhere.

"Fortunately 'a rose by any other name would smell as sweet,' and nothing could injure the economic qualities of the Buff Orpington, which proved to be very great.

"No breed of fowl has attained so universal a popularity, in spite of the many disqualifications met with.

"The demand for these birds grew so rapidly that it was impossible to meet it.

"Large numbers of half-breed Buff Cochins and Dorkings were sold as Buff Orpingtons.

"We have seen the progeny of high-priced birds sold as pure stock, of which 75 per cent were yellow-legged and feather-legged. Anything bearing the name 'Buff Orpington' was saleable, or as a Lincolnshire breeder wrote us, 'If I call my birds Lincolnshire Buff, I cannot get more than 4s. each for them; if I call them Buff Orpingtons, they readily sell at 10s. each.'

"But that stage has passed. At first the resemblance between the Blacks and Buffs was more imaginary than real. Now the latter are longer in leg and more upright.

"But the different types have been brought nearer together. Even yet there is a tendency to yellow and feathered legs, but not nearly to the extent met with formerly."

White Orpingtons

Mr. Cook claimed to have originated the white variety by crossing White Leghorn males with Black Hamburg pullets. The pullets from this cross that came white were mated to White Dorking males.

The following diagram will perhaps give a better idea of how the various crosses were used.

White Orpington	White Dorking Male		
	Leghorn-Hamburg Cross	White Leghorn Male	
		Black Hamburg Pullets	

In spite of the above claim, many English breeders claim that the Whites are sports from the Blacks.

Judging from the size and type of the Whites seen in our American shows, I do not see how this could be possible, as they seem of a different type entirely, although during the past two years the type of the three varieties seems to be getting more uniform.

The Rose Comb White was produced in the same manner as the Single Comb, the only difference being that a Rose Comb Dorking was used instead of a single comb, according to the information received from Mr. P. A. Cook.

Diamond Jubilee Orpingtons

Mr. Cook claimed to have originated this variety and we have never heard the claim disputed. They were given the name "Diamond Jubilee Orpingtons" as they were brought out in 1897 during Queen Victoria's Diamond Jubilee. One of the best pens was presented to the late Queen. She was an ardent poultry fancier and on her estate was to be found a fine, up-to-date poultry plant.

Mr. P. A. Cook says: "The Jubilee Orpingtons were produced by mating the same breeds together as were used in the Buff Orpingtons, only a Speckled Dorking was used instead of a colored one, this being used for the last cross."

The Jubilee Orpingtons have never been very popular; why, we cannot say. They are a three-colored fowl. The ground or main color is a rich, reddish brown, then a black bar, which is usually a beetle green and then tipped with white.

Spangled Orpingtons

Mr. Cook also claimed to be the originator of the Spangled variety and produced them by crossing a dark or colored Dorking cock with Barred Plymouth Rock hens. The pullets from this cross were of large size and mostly black. These were mated with a Silver Spangled Hamburg cock.

Of course it took some time after this to perfect the color, as the males were inclined to come drab or straw color. The Spangled Orpingtons are a black and white fowl, the feathers are black, tipped or spangled with white. They are not, as yet, a very popular fowl.

Blue Orpingtons

Blue Orpingtons made their appearance at English shows last season and are most likely a cross of the Whites and Blacks.

Ermine or Columbian Orpingtons

Ermine Orpingtons were originated by Angier L. Goodwin of Melrose Highlands, Mass., and first exhibited by him at the Boston Show of 1909. They were produced from accidental crosses of the Black, White and Buff Orpington varieties. The color markings are the same as those of Light Brahmas, which lead other breeders of new varieties to make Orpington-Light Brahma crosses for the purpose of producing a Columbian Orpington, which is identical in color markings with the Ermine Orpington.

Cuckoo Orpingtons

The newest of the Orpington family is the above variety, introduced in 1901 (?) by William H. Cook of England, but none have been exhibited in America, that we are aware of.

Admitted to the Standard

Single and Rose Comb Black and Single and Rose Comb Buff Orpingtons were admitted to the English Poultry Club Standard in 1901. The American Poultry Association admitted the Single Comb Buff, Black and White Orpingtons to the Standard of Perfection in 1904.

CHAPTER II

Orpington Type

Variations of Shape and Breed Characteristics in Black, Buff and White Orpingtons—Comparison of
American and English Standard Types—Chart Illustrations Showing the Correct Cobby
Type of the Orpington—English Type of the Past and Present Illustrated

J. H. Drevenstedt

HAPE makes the breed; color the variety" is an old familiar expression coined by F. B. Zimmer twenty years or more ago. It has been used ever since by writers on Standard bred poultry because it most briefly and emphatically defines the type of all varieties bearing the family name of the breed as being the same for all. This is, or should be the Standard law for all breeds recognized by the American Poultry Association and the English Poultry Club.

When we speak or write about Plymouth Rock, Wyandotte, Rhode Island Red or Leghorn type we have in mind only the ideal Standard shape of the breed. There can, or should be no difference in the shape of the White, Barred, Buff, or Penciled Plymouth Rocks, even if some Barred and White Plymouth Rock faddists are at odds over what the correct type should be. Individual preference in such cases is departing from a universal Standard accepted by all breeders as a rule, and ignored by a few who have a type of their own strain. Compare the winning specimens of the Barred Plymouth Rocks with those of the White, Buff and Penciled varieties and departure from Standard Plymouth Rock type in the former will be far more frequent than in the latter. Barred Plymouth Rock fanciers have gravitated toward the Wyandotte type as the Standard illustration of the Barred Plymouth Rock male clearly shows. The breeders of other varieties have adhered more closely to the correct type and have not sacrificed shape for color. The remarkable evenness in type of White Plymouth Rocks seen at our leading shows is a convincing illustration of Zimmer's old saying, "Shape makes the breed; color the variety." We make the above comparison of Plymouth Rock types because in a similar, but greater degree, the Orpingtons are affected. The original Orpington is the Single Comb Black. All other varieties of the Orpington family are such in name only. There is no blood relationship between the latter and the Simon-pure Black Orpington, except in the case of the Rose Comb Black, the latter having a Rose Comb Langshan male progenitor instead of a Single Comb Langshan. Some strains of White Orpingtons are claimed to be white sports of the Single Comb Blacks, which, if true, should entitle them to the claim of being true Orpingtons in the blood lines and also claim heritage to the massive type of the original Orpington. With the knowledge of the origin of each variety of Orpington as given in the previous chapter, it is readily understood why there is such a variation in type in Black, Buff and White varieties. To look at the three classes exhibited at shows several years ago, no disinterested observer would have thought the Buffs and Whites belonged to the Orpington family, the type being distinct in each from that of the Black Orpingtons. In the last two years the type of the

Whites has greatly improved, the best specimens exhibited rivaling the Blacks in massiveness and size and approaching closely the outline of the original type. So, also, in a lesser degree have the Buffs gradually approached the Blacks in size and type but there is still much room for improvement in this respect, as hundreds of Buff Orpingtons, albeit sound and beautiful in color, are too long in shank, too narrow in breast and lacking depth and length of body, breadth of back and fullness of

EARLY ENGLISH BLACK ORPINGTONS

The above illustration appeared in the book "The Orpington and Its Varieties" by E. Campbell and represents the Orpington type of that day. The influence of Langshan blood is readily noticeable in the shape lines of the back and tail of the female and to a lesser degree in the shape of the tail of the male. The fullness of the neck and the depth of the body are, however, characteristic of the original Black Orpington.— Editor.

hackle and tail. They resemble the Rock more than they do the Orpington type. But here is the same old rock which Plymouth Rock breeders have struck in their path to uniformity of type, many breeders of Buff Orpingtons desire a longer shanked and bodied bird than possessed by the Black Orpington of today. They find it difficult to obtain the size, massiveness of body and the profusion of feathering characteristic of the modern Black Orpington, also believing the latter has been allowed to depart from the original type of the Cook Orpingtons introduced twenty years ago. A study of the illustrations— Figures 1 and 2 of Chapter I—will show the original type in 1890. The illustration on this page shows the English type of 1902.

General Shape, Carriage and Plumage

In the English Standard the above is described as follows: "Cobby and compact; erect and graceful; plumage close." In the American Standard of 1905 Orpingtons are described as follows: "Large and stately in appearance, with long round deep bodies and very full breast and back development. The abundance of hackle and saddle feathers on the Orpington male gives him the appearance of having a short back, whereas it is both broad and long like that in the female Orpington."

The revised American Standard of 1910, gives substantially the same description as the one of 1905, but in clearer and more detailed language placing particular importance on the maintenance of the cobby type, which the original English Orpington possessed. In other words: Keep away from the loose fluffy feathered Cochin body and thighs seen on some strains of Black and White Orpingtons which have been "sized up" by the introduction of Cochin blood. The English carriage horse, the Cob, with his fine head, strong full arched neck, deep, full and rounded, albeit compact, body, is the correct idea of what constitutes the cobby type in horses, and this in a corresponding and modified degree, can be applied to the accepted and correct type of the Orpington fowl.

English Standard Type.

The illustration on the opposite page represents the ideal English Standard type of Orpingtons. It was drawn by J. W. Ludlow, England's greatest poultry artist now living, and printed in Lewis Wright's comprehensive and invaluable publication "The New Book of Poultry" 1902, Cassell & Co. Limited, London, Paris and New York, from which we reproduce it.

Comparison of English and American Standards

Comparisons may be odious, as the old saying goes, but frequently, when applied to Standard type variation, may prove more instructive and interesting that otherwise. To fix in the minds of our breeders the true and original type of the Orpington, no better method than the comparison of the American and English Standards can be presented to the student of form. Consequently, we reproduce in the "deadly parallel columns" below the shape variations as found in the English Standard of 1901 and the American Standards of 1905 and 1910.

STANDARD SHAPE OF ORPINGTON MALE

Section	English Standard 1901	American Standard 1905	American Standard 1910
Head	Small, neat, fairly full over eye	Medium	Rather large
Beak	Strong and nicely curved	Short, stout, regularly curved	Short, stout, regularly curved
Eyes	Full, bright, intelligent	Large	Large
Comb	Medium	Medium size in proportion to specimen	Rather large
Ear-lobes	Medium size, rather long	Medium size	Medium size
Wattles	Medium	Medium size	Medium
Neck	Nicely curved, abundant hackle	Medium length, large, well arched, abundant hackle	Rather short, well arched, abundant hackle
Back	Short with broad shoulders, saddle rising slightly	Broad, long, rising with slight concave sweep to tail.	Broad, medium with full concave sweep to tail
Breast	Broad, deep and full, carried well forward, long straight breast bone	Broad, deep, full	Broad, deep, well rounded
Body	Note: In English Standard the Body section includes breast, back, saddle and wings.—Ed.	Long, broad, deep keel, bone rather long, straight, extending well forward	Broad, deep; keel bone rather long, extending well forward
Wings	Well formed, carried close to body	Medium, well folded	Medium, well folded
Tail	Medium in size, flowing and inclined backward	Medium length, fairly well spread; carried at an angle of 45 degrees	Moderately long, fairly well spread; carried at an angle of 45 degrees
Legs and Toes	Thighs short; shanks short and strong Toes—4 in number, well spread	Thighs large, rather short; shanks short. Toes of medium length, straight, strong, well spread	Thighs large, rather short; shanks short, stout in bone Toes of medium length, straight, strong, well spread

STANDARD TYPE OF ORPINGTON FEMALE

Section	English Standard 1901	American Standard 1905	American Standard 1910
Head, Comb and Neck	As in the male	As in the male	As in the male
Breast	As in the male	As in the male	As in the male
Back, Wings and Body	Cushion: small but sufficient to give back a short and graceful curved appearance	As in the male	Neck: Tapering to head, hackle moderately full Back: Broad moderately long, rising with concave sweep to tail
Tail	Medium size, inclined backward and upward	Carried at an angle of 40 degrees	Carried at an angle of 40 degrees
Legs and Toes	As in the male	As in the male	As in the male

Evolution of Orpington Ideals in America

A. O. Schilling, who has made a careful study of Orpington type at our leading poultry shows and examined and handled many specimens in prominent breeders' yards, in the Reliable Poultry Journal, July, 1910, clearly illustrates the evolution of Orpington ideals in America by pen and ink drawings with explanatory remarks, which are reproduced as follows:

"We desire to show by the accompanying cuts and this short article the variation or changes in the ideals that have from time to time pleased the fanciers. A little study of the accompanying pen and ink illustration will show what has been done to the Orpington type by American breeders. On pages 22 and 23 we show a pair of ideal Buff Orpingtons drawn to conform to the ideal of their originators, Wm. Cook & Sons, and of other prominent breeders of that time, which was prior to the revision of the Standard of 1905. It will be noticed that this type is much shorter in body, which emphasizes its great depth and the fullness of the breast and it shows to good advantage the U-shape in body and back of male, which was an expression used by the late Wm. Cook in describing the typical Orpington. It is quite evident that breeders on this side of the Atlantic are striving to produce a longer bodied bird than was originally advocated. In Figs. A and B we have illustrated the difference in type between the earlier ideal and the present-day Standard Orpington.

"There has been some discussion among prominent breeders in regard to the advisability of doing away with the short shank and thigh of the present-day ideal, mainly for the reason that it will not fit the Buff variety. Whether or not this will be done or whether it will benefit the breed or the breeders, remains to be seen. In the writer's opinion an ideal that fits one variety should also fit all varieties of the breed in order to enable us to have a Standard that will not be open to criticism and productive of much argument.

"Even though we have an accepted standard and ideal which meets the approval of a large majority, differences of opinion will always exist in regard to standard poultry as well as in other matters, but we shall aim to show in the forthcoming Standard an ideal that will represent the modern Orpington as it is exhibited by the most successful breeders in this country.

"We have in our possession photographic studies of many prominent winning specimens in nearly all varieties of Orpingtons that have been shown at the greatest exhibitions held in this country for a number of years and the new Standard ideal will be a composite made from the ideal parts of the best specimens shown in recent years. These ideals will be submitted to the specialty clubs for approval before final adoption by the American Poultry Association at the next annual meeting.

"There is no doubt in our minds that adding to the length of body which seems to be the general tendency in most of our American breeds today, has been of benefit

STANDARD BLACK ORPINGTONS. ENGLISH TYPES

Illustration is reproduced from "The New Book of Poultry," by Lewis Wright, published in 1902 by Cassell & Company, Limited, London, Paris and New York. Delineation is by J. W. Ludlow, England's best poultry artist now living. The Standard shape of all varieties of Orpington fowls is identical, male and female respectively, therefore this picture gives the English type or shape outline of all the Orpingtons, as interpreted by Mr. Ludlow.

EARLY IDEAL ORPINGTON MALE

to the breed and we find the specimens approaching nearest our Standard ideals for Orpington type, fowls of
beauty and usefulness."

Type Variation in English Orpingtons

In his excellent book "The Orpington and Its Varieties" London, England, 1908, the author, E. Campbell, fur-

nishes the following interesting comparison of the differences in Single Comb Black and Single Comb Buff Orpington types: "Although it is generally accepted in theory
that there is nothing but color to distinguish the two
varieties, there are in reality very great and material differences. In type for instance, a difficulty in Black is to
keep the tail within its symmetrical limits, for if ill bred it
generally develops quite a large and high pitched tail. In
the Buff, on the other hand, a difficulty is to get sufficient
tail with a broad enough feather.

"Type in Blacks insists on a short leg and a square,
massive, well let-down body. Type in Buffs at the moment
is almost a minor matter, and you can go to any leading
show and find half-a-dozen different types carded—color in
feather mostly determining the awards.

"Size, too, is a *sine qua non* in Blacks. It only comes
into the judging of Buffs when birds are otherwise level
as to color and type.

"For these reasons Buffs, as a whole, do not exhibit
that grand massiveness and bulk which one can find in
the best Blacks. But now that the value of type has been
given a proper place in the Buff Orpington Standard, we
may hope for an improvement, for size follows type in the
breed as certainly as day follows night.

"It is urged that the buff color is so difficult to secure
that its value from a breeder's point of view far transcends
type or size, and no one who has bred Buffs will deny the
great cogency of this argument. But many thoughtful
lovers of the breed have, like myself, deplored the extreme lengths to which some breeders have gone, and
which some judges have sanctioned, in search of purity of
plumage alone. I have seen a Buff Dorking cockerel, so
far as type and characteristics go, even at the Dairy
Show, and, truth to tell, he had to win or the judge, himself a sound Buff breeder, would have been attacked from
every quarter.

"The very pronounced advance made in color, within
the last couple of years, has so altered the situation that
I think the Buff breeder who loses sight of type and size
may find himself awkwardly situated.

"As black breeders know it is very difficult indeed to
breed in type and size. As a rule it is not attempted, be-

A and B. Composite outline drawings of Orpington male and female, illustrating the difference between the accepted American Standard ideal and the early U-shape type of body. The dotted lines show the type that was in favor
some five years ago. The heavy lines show the type of bird that finds favor with the best breeders and judges of the
present day.—A. O. Schilling.

cause it is cheaper, easier, and more satisfactory to get fresh blood and start afresh. Should it occur, as is not improbable, that type and size shall be demanded as imperatively in Buffs as in Blacks, then the breeder who has neglected these points will find himself out of the running for some time.

"To secure feather color, in-and-in-breeding has been resorted to by some breeders, with such success that in many instances long backed and narrow chested types have been so fixed that their prepotency is very strong, and they will resist change accordingly and revert back in a most irritating manner.

"That in-breeding of this sort is absolutely necessary to secure color we have been told by some authorities, and their success shows that it is sound in practice at least. But that it has been retained by more than one noted Buff breeder who indulges in fresh blood each season for his best pen so as to maintain type, substance and stamina, is proof to me at least that although a ready method it is not quite indispensable. And as it brings other dangers in its train, only dire necessity can justify it—such a necessity as is gradually being swept away by the general advance towards a pure Buff feather."

The Goodacre Chart

A. G. Goodacre of California, one of the earliest breeders and importers of Orpingtons, who was associated with Mr. Willett in the east at the beginning of the Orpington boom in America, contributed an instructive chart representing Orpington type to the National Single Comb Buff Orpington Club catalog of 1906 which we reproduce here.

Mr. Goodacre offers the following explanation of the above chart:

"We give a chart showing an Orpington pullet, the inner dotted line where the actual carcass of the bird is carried. This aptly illustrates how the back of an Orpington is shortened by a slight cushion, a strong hackle and a

rather short, neat tail; where the dotted line approaches the superficial line the feathers will be found shorter; the typical Orpington has a long under line and a medium long back; the great length of body has been moulded in such a way as to cover up harsh lines on the surface and stamped it with a character entirely different to all other breeds of poultry. We desire a rather long tapering head, with very prominent eyes, a comb in proportion to the specimen, medium in size with five serrations, arched so that the spikes point uniformly outward; the largest spike in the center, the others shortening to outer edges. The comb should have a good broad base setting well on skull, the neck hackle full, in the males a continuation of lustrous feathers from head to tail, not broken across the shoulders with coarser feathers; the saddle should be full, and tail medium in male; the tail in female should rise gradually from back, being rather short and pinched; both sexes should show great depth from back to hock, the shanks rather short with toes apparently long, a broad back across shoulders, flat, with a deep well rounded breast, coupled with an arched neck, good red lobes and wattles, a sprightly walk, and always that great depth of body at any angle viewed. These are the characteristics of a fowl with a strong constitution, and the Orpington everybody wants; the commercial fowl as well as the show bird."

This chart is an excellent object lesson for those, who year in and year out, keep advocating long backs on fowls and condemning short ones, as well as the blocky or cobby type of Orpingtons and other breeds. These critics judge the length of back by the feathered outline and not by the carcass line. Feathers like religion, cover up a multitude of bad qualities, but they frequently also hide the good ones. But feathers, when perfectly developed in each section, fix the type of the breed as unmistakably as two and two make four. It is but another illustration of the old truism: "Shape makes the breed and color the variety."

EARLY IDEAL ORPINGTON FEMALE

Evolution of English Types of Langshans, Orpingtons and Cochins

An Interesting and Valuable Study of the Relative Types of Three Allied Breeds with Sketches
Showing Changes in Shape During the Past Thirty-Five Years

J. W. Ludlow, England

MY idea in drawing attention to these three varieties of poultry is to show the alliance, progress and gradual development which has taken place within the past thirty-five years.

As I am about to write from memory, I may not be strictly accurate in dates. I suppose it is about thirty-five or forty years since the introduction of the first Langshans into this country. Anyhow, about that period Black Cochins (never a large number, owing to the stupid insistence of yellow legs and beak) had run down to almost total extinction. There were but few fanciers who were willing to make an effort to breed up to an ideal so exacting as a big, bulky, squat, heavily feathered Black Cochin with yellow legs and beak. The object was too much of an unreality, yielding so small a percentage of progeny anywhere approaching the desired yellow leg and beak points, together with the massive fluffy proportions, such as attained, and more easily, in the more naturally produced Buffs.

Thus Black Cochins were at that period a comparatively used-up, puny, neglected sort, and remained so until the advent of Langshans, at which time a ray of hope shone upon the few scattered remnants. The idea of a "cross" between our British Black Chinee and his newly-imported brother (the Croad Langshan) soon took root, and it was not long ere the influence of this harmonious union became apparent not by yellow leg and beak. Oh, no! That color anomaly had to be abandoned, and rightly so, for it had already been a too serious impediment in the way of Black Cochin breeding to be longer insisted upon as a standard feature.

Fifty years ago the few Black Cochins we had were in the main narrow, flat-sided, half-breeds in appearance, not good enough to class with the Buffs nor numerous enough to be called a strain. They were chiefly "sports," inevitable variations from the early day, less purified, but pedigreed, mixed-color stocks—the days when Buffs were anything from cinnamon to yellow, with black tails, flights, foot-feather, and black-striped hackle. From such as these, blacks came occasionally, whether wanted or not, as did also whites, partridge and cuckoos. "Buffs," being the grand centerpiece of attraction, were "all the go." Buff, buff, buff was the craze then with Cochins, as it is now with Buff Orpingtons. The same questions were asked then as now as to "exact shade of color" preferred.

It has been my lot and my pleasure to watch these changes from the very earliest period to the Cochin era, even to the fulfillment of one's hopes and expectations, as exemplified in the ideal specimens of the Buffs of today, in which the names of Tomlinson, Proctor, Felton, Bailey, Wade, Bagshaw, and Riddell will long remain most prominent, as will also the names of Chase and Darby for Whites, Harriss, Southon, and Felton for Partridge, and Colonel Williamson and the Rev. Dodd for Blacks, the variety to which my notes especially apply.

So great is the change which has taken place in Buff Cochins in fifty years that I feel almost tempted to depict and describe the wonderful alteration in them also, but my theme here is Blacks only and their alliance with Croad Langshans, and, as a sequence, at least a link also with the Black Orpington.

What I particularly want to show is that the best Black Cochins of today are in perfect line in point of size, fluffy massiveness, heavy foot-feathering and general Cochin rotundity and other all-round characteristics, well up in all good points, level, or nearly so, with their brethren, the magnificent Buffs of today. Such a raising of the standard Black has only been possible by reason of the skillful infusion of the thickest set, shortest legged Langshans of thirty-five years ago. Today the extraordinary massive features of George Proctor's Buffs and Colonel Williamson's Blacks each can toe the line of equality, each models of excellence, neither having any point needing improvement.

It is not pleasant, perhaps, to be told that one's stock is the result of a "cross." It is preferable to regard them as pure and undefiled, clear of the mongrelizing element, but in this case there is none of the "mongrel" in the alliance—none whatever. It has been simply the bringing together of long-parted strains of the same tribe, and I conceive there is far more credit due in working a strain up to perfection in accord with the generally accepted model than working at a ready-made type until they degenerate in constitution and points of merit. If in the exposition of these alliances I offend any Langshan, Orpington, or Black Cochin breeders, I am sorry, but I am writing from an experience extending over sixty years' watchful, practical experience. I have seen many ideas put into practice, and have lived long enough to have seen most of them worked out to perfection.

If you look at the illustration on the opposite page, take the top row, note the (No. 1) Croad Langshan to the left, and then see present-day British 1910 type to the extreme right (No. 6). The difference is great, but the object is clearly achieved.

Look again at the middle row, "Orpingtons" (7 to 12). Many fanciers objected to the scanty foot-feathering of the Langshans. It was said to be neither one thing nor the other. So clean-legged strains were soon started, leading up from leggy No. 7, on the left, and finishing off with the up-to-date short-legged ideal as depicted on center line to the right (No. 12).

Then take the bottom row, Black Cochins. The meagre-looking No. 13 to the left represents one of the best of a poor lot in 1875, and those not reliable for reproduction. Compare him with the modern type of bird on the right (18), and you will realize there has been something more than theory in the scheme.

To the late William Cook is rightly ascribed the credit of producing and naming the Black Orpington. Certainly he brought them out, named them, and kept them up in prominence until their merits and value were fully assured. Then they went up by leaps and bounds in popularity. The contest for supremacy was strong between such staunch breeders as the ever genial Cook himself, Johnstone, Peele, Bell, Partington, Cross

EVOLUTION OF ENGLISH TYPES OF LANGSHANS, ORPINGTONS AND COCHINS.

A pictorial record of thirty-five years at intervals of seven years. Nos. 1, 7, and 13 show the original types, and 6, 12, and 18 the up-to-date ideal. These illustrations were drawn by the eminent English artist, J. W. Ludlow, and appeared in connection with his explanatory article in the Feathered World, England, September 2, 1910. We are indebted to the latter excellent poultry journal for the reprints of both illustrations and the article.—Editor.

Brothers, Bloomer, Hallam and Litting, Galway, Fawkes, Lewis, and many other enthusiasts. In fact, there has been a lot of money spent on Orpingtons, and although Blacks are now stationary, they are ready to rise again when the Buff craze has somewhat subsided, and when Whites have advanced a bit.

By-the-bye, Blacks being the safest occasional cross for the produce of bulky Whites it will become necessary to carefully examine and guard against grizzly under-fluff in all and any of the black progeny thus produced. An occasional dip is good, over-much leads to spoil the glossy splendor and produce a dull black plumage. In fact, the advantage is to the Whites only to the detriment of the Blacks thus crossed. I name this because I know that, in the effort to get size, bulk, and character

in Whites, some of the biggest Blacks have been and are being used for the purpose.

Returning, however, to the kernel of the nut—viz., the alliance, progress and severance of these three sorts— those of the old brigade, like myself, who remember the first imported Cochins, and thirty-five years later the first draft of Langshans, and still later the making of Black Orpingtons, may have solved the problem of descent for themselves, and therefore probably will regard these notes as unnecessary, but in the interval there has sprung up a new generation of fanciers, who, less experienced, would be justified in doubting the alliance of these three up-to-dates, Nos. 6, 12 and 18, which have now become so dissimilar in structural points as to baffle those of limited experience as to their pedigree.

FIRST PRIZE PEN OF WHITE ORPINGTONS AT BOSTON, 1910.

Owned and Bred by Owen Farms, Vineyard Haven, Mass.

I have heard the British bred Langshans described as Ostriches, as Storks, as Malay-crossed, because of their abnormally long legs. I have heard and also read of the Black Orpington being the result of crosses with the Minorca, the Java, and the Black Rock (I could accept a judicious infusion of the latter), but in the whole course of my experience have never observed even a suspicion of Minorca in .their composition. I have also heard it suggested in the usual strictly confidential whisper that Mr. So-and-So obtained his brilliant green sheen by a cross with the Black Hamburgh! Well, when one hears such stuff uttered by young men or chattering professors, it seems in the face of such ignorance excusable in me to expose the real position.

I have seen pure-bred Langshans, both Croad and modern, with red feathers in hackle and saddle. Personally I did not look upon these blemishes as indicative of outside or alien color cross. Certainly not; if there are not such occasional reversions how are we to expect a maintenance of the brilliant sheeny plumage so essential a finish to an otherwise tip-top specimen? Some would say, "Ah, this is a bit of the Malay coming out, this is!" Others perhaps, with a wink of cunning, would suggest it as sight influence, owing to close proximity to an adjoining pen of colored fowls.

The late Major and Miss Croad denounced the red feather as no part of their—"the true"—strain; but they had it all the same in some of their best birds, and need not have been ashamed to admit the fact, for such reversions come occasionally in the purest of well-established strains. The profound student in his search for true permanent characteristics has to look deeper for proofs of lineage than a few or even many red feathers in a green-sheened Black strain.

As an artist and judge of vast experience, extending over sixty years, I have carefully watched the evolution of these three sorts from the beginning of their history; have studied every little detail of their composition, from the egg to the chick, their habits, their growth, their structure, their flesh, skin, and fat, their expression, the texture, wrinkles or puckers in their faces, even to the deep-toned gutteral, gurgling sound of their crow, and I find them each and all more or less partaking of the same heavy Asiatic characteristics,—enough to stamp them as members, it may be, of various near or distant strains or families, but certainly of one and the same tribe or origin.

Well, it may be said, what good end has been served in thus . severing and purifying and raising each to exhibition dignity? It is only adding more to the already over-purified "fancy poultry." Yes, a good deal might be said on this score, more than I can explain in these brief notes. There has been much said of late for the "utility" side of poultry culture, very much good done by able advocates of that special branch, but if we are to make real permanent progress we must look to both sides of the subject. Personally, I hold the exhibition side to be of first consideration, as an absolute necessity, as a means, perhaps the only means, of making sure of success in the greater, the national, section. It is out of the "fancy" stocks (the perfected, pedigreed, tabulated types) that one can look to from time to time for reliable "crosses" for the produce of the strictly speaking "utilitarian" market poultry.

The illustration (sketch and notes) of these three sorts should furnish a fair example of what can be done by unity of effort in the right direction. It is one of the many instances in which much has been got out of nothing. Three distinct classes and types of high-class, valuable show birds have been obtained from plain, common-place looking ancestors, a distinct gain to the nation, to say nothing of the immense pleasure and profit gained by the multitude of fanciers who have from time to time taken their parts in these praiseworthy, interesting, useful, and profitable pursuits.

Type Variations

Comparison of Buff and White Orpington Shape with that of Black Orpingtons—The New Standard Type the Correct Ideal for All Three Varieties

M. F. Delano

THE above topic is one that gives me the greatest pleasure to write about, and it should appeal very strongly to every thinking breeder in the United States. A variety is made or marred by the correctness of the ideal type which is established for that breed. There have been instances galore where grand good breeds and varieties have been absolutely ruined as utility birds by breeders taking as their ideal a type sufficiently different from the one nature intended for the variety to impair and ruin their utility qualities. In considering the future type of the Orpington it is the earnest desire of the writer that we make progress in type one that will allow us not only to retain but improve the wonderful utility qualities of the Orpington fowl today.

The Blacks were the first of the Orpingtons to be brought before the public. They were a grand, big fowl, profusely and loosely feathered, inheriting the latter characteristic from their Cochin ancestors. They had all of the fine qualities of the Langshan and the other heavy laying blood that went into their make-up and were naturally low down and close to the ground, and this characteristic appealed to the fanciers and they tried to make it an inherent one in the variety as a whole and bred with this ideal in view.

In the course of time the Buff variety and then the White were brought before the public and placed on the market and they were given the same name and called Orpingtons. The blood that went into the make-up of these two latter varieties was widely differing from that from which the Black was formed. They had been given the same name and therefore it was deemed necessary to breed them to the same type. So for years the fanciers on this side of the water have been endeavoring to bring about this result. In England they have not demanded the same type in the Buff and the White possessed by the Black, but have developed the two latter varieties along normal lines to make them the grand utility fowl that have become pre-eminent in England over all other varieties and have taken a leading place in France as well.

The American Poultry Association has admitted three varieties of the Orpington to our American Standard of Perfection, the Buff, Black and White Single Comb varieties. The rest of the varieties of Orpingtons that have been placed on the market have never proven generally popular and no concerted action has been taken to get any of them admitted to the Standard. Each one of the varieties has been made up of different blood lines and no two varieties naturally have exactly the same type. There are specimens in each of the varieties that approach very closely to the best of the Blacks in type but they are not plentiful, and a great many of the leading Orpington breeders feel that the Standard requirements have been made too stringent for the future good of the Buff and White varieties, and for that reason the present Standard was a little modified at the Niagara Falls and St. Louis meetings of the American Poultry Association and the new Standard will have an ideal picture more normal and nearer the true ideal for the average Orpington.

With few exceptions the extremely large, low down birds have not been remarkably good layers, whether their color has been black, buff or white. The females a trifle higher on legs, with good long bodies and plenty of depth, have made the producers, and this is the type that is becoming more and more popular as time goes on. The Buffs and the Whites are the most popular varieties and probably always will be, and it is not right to make them suffer because they were not bred from the same sources as were the Blacks.

There is no better utility fowl today than the Orpington. There is no handsomer fowl, or a fowl that is more fascinating for the gentleman fancier or the painstaking breeder, and their future is absolutely safe when bred along the conservative lines required under the new Standard. The writer predicts that their present popularity is almost nothing to what they will attain as time goes on and that the birds themselves have the intrinsic merit to hold their place as one of the four leading breeds of America.

ENGLISH TYPE WHITE ORPINGTONS, 1908

CHAPTER III

Black Orpingtons

Exhibition and Market Qualities—Mating for Size and Shape—Breeding for Color—Comments and Contributions by Noted English Authorities and American Breeders

J. H. Drevenstedt

HE Blacks being the first of the Orpingtons to arrive in the poultry world, they must be accorded the priority claim in the chapters on the different varieties of Orpingtons, regardless of their rank in popularity among Orpington breeders. They gave the family name to the breed and deserve the honor.

When we first judged and handled Orpingtons some eight or nine years ago, the Blacks impressed us the most, being distinct in type, grand in size and beautiful in the color of the plumage, the latter, at least in the best specimens, we handled at that time, having the rich beetle green sheen so much fancied by all breeders of Black Hamburgs and Black Langshans. A Black Orpington cockerel and pullet hatched in April, and exhibited by Mr. Kerr at Newark, N. J., in December of the same year, filled their cages, so to speak, the immense size of these massive youngsters being a revelation to all poultry breeders present. There has been no diminution in size since that early period, the Black Orpingtons of today being fully as large and massive, if not larger, than the early comers from across the seas. Their immense size and beautiful color caught the fancy of many conservative breeders, the plack plumage being no handicap in this instance. The importations grew in volume and it did not take long before the choicest feathered specimens from the yards of Cook, Partington and Bell found their way to the United States and Canada.

Exhibition and Market Qualities

The origin of Black Orpingtons has been given in a previous chapter, but the evolution of the different strains and the value of the breed as a utility fowl remain to be presented. We can seek no better source for authentic information relating to the matter than in the land of its birth. The late Lewis Wright, in his great work "The New Book of Poultry," treats this subject in a clear and authoritative manner, so that the following extracts from his comprehensive chapter on the Orpington fowl will prove valuable and interesting to American breeders:

"There is no doubt that some original Black Orpingtons were produced as stated; but there is as little doubt that the breed has since considerably changed in two distinct directions. As stated in our next chapter, there is little question that one of the components of the Plymouth Rock was the Black Java fowl; and as stated in the preceding, it is equally obvious that this Black Java has much in common with the Langshan, however that fact be interpreted. This darker and more typical component in the Asiatic blood had thus a double prepotency, and its predominance over the more Shanghai component would be intensified by breeding for clean instead of feathered shanks. This doubly strong element therefore rapidly overpowered the Minorca element, and the Orpingtons quickly became to all intents and purposes clean-legged

Langshans, taking the place of that shorter-legged, symmetrical type once popular, but subsequently discarded by the personal feeling of the Langshan breeders. In addition to this mere tendency, however, it is within our own personal knowledge that clean-legged pure Langshans, from perfectly orthodox sources, were sold to Orpington exhibitors, and appeared immediately in exhibition pens,

"LADY WASHINGTON"

Black Orpington hen, winner of first prize at Madison Square Garden, New York, 1909-10, pronounced by Judge Oke the most typical Orpington in the show. Reproduced from photograph furnished by Black Diamond Poultry Farm.

as well as being used for breeding with their stock. This still further strengthened and hastened the reversion to Langshan type, which has been so pronounced that at many shows only one class for 'Langshan or Orpington' (or the converse) has been provided for the two breeds. The index of this change has lain chiefly in the size of the eggs, which has somewhat lessened since the Minorca element lost power; and in the color of the eyes, which was often red while any foreign element remained, but has now almost everywhere reverted to the Langshan brown or black.

"There has been, however, quite another change, a Black Orpington of practically new blood coming upon the scene about 1891. In that year Mr. Joseph Partington exhibited at the Dairy Show in October two cockerels and two pullets, which secured first and second prizes in each class, three of the four birds being immediately sold at £30 each; notwithstanding which at the Palace Show a few weeks later he brought out fresh birds of each sex that beat these previous winners. These birds were of a size that had never before been seen, creating quite a sensation and considerable curiosity. Mr. Partington assures us that these Orpingtons also were cross-made birds, but had none whatever, of Mr. Cook's original strain in them at all, and that he had deliberately started with the idea of breeding himself something in the same line, but more striking and handsome. They were very large, and of splendid color, with massive shape, and all had dark eyes. These points made them invincible in the show pen, and the new strain soon spread all over the country, and also abroad, and has supplied most of the winners of the present day. Many of the birds display so much more fluff than former Black Orpingtons, that we cannot help thinking large females of either Black, White or perhaps even

SIR BEETLE

WINNER OF FIRST PRIZE, MADISON SQ. GARDEN,
NEW YORK 1909-1910.
BRED AND OWNED BY FOXHURST FARM LIME ROCK CONN U S A

Buff Cochin, may have been employed with Langshan males. Mr. Partington describes this type of the breed as follows:

'Black Orpingtons are really a very useful breed of birds. They are very handsome, good layers, and one of the best for table use. They always look well all the year 'round, as they never lose their color. They will do well in either small or open runs, being a very hardy bird; but they will not stand heavy feeding.

'The color of the cock should be a rich green black; beak either black or dark horn with a dark eye. He should have a firm straight comb, not over large. The back should not be too long, and tail not too large; legs not long, the thigh just showing; weight 9 lbs. to 11 lbs. The color of the hen

WINNER OF FIRST, MADISON SQUARE GARDEN, NEW YORK 1908-09
BRED AND OWNED BY FOXHURST FARM, LIME ROCK, CONN U S A

is the same, and similar remarks apply as to her back. tail and legs; her weight should be 7 lbs. to 10 lbs.'

Breeding Black Orpingtons

"Color should be bred for as in the Langshan, but the crimson between the toes is not required. Particular attention should be given to preserving the correct shape, with a broad and deep breast, the whole body looking massive and solid, and set rather low. Excessive fluff should be avoided, as tending to decrease laying, and being often accompanied by thicker skin; too small combs, also, are apt to be signs of diminished egg production. We have seen one or two specimens distinctly keeled, almost like some exhibition ducks, and this ought certainly to be deprecated. It is probably due to carelessness of these points, that statements have lately appeared to the effect that some strains of the Black Orpington have not kept up its reputation as a good layer. Both abundance and size of eggs would, however, quickly respond to selection for these qualities, in the manner insisted upon in former chapters of this work.

"It is not at all necessary in Black Orpingtons to mate different pens for breeding cockerels and pullets; typical birds of good color on both sides will produce in their turn exhibition specimens."

Breeding for Color

To produce the proper greenish black color of Orpingtons is one of the problems that breeders in England and America are called upon to solve each succeeding breeding season. Although sound color in Blacks may be considered by many fanciers less difficult to produce than in Buffs, it is safe to assert, that the Black Orpingtons produced with absolutely sound black plumage having lustrous greenish black sheen on the surface, free from any trace of purple barring, are just as scarce and as difficult to breed as an absolutely sound Buff Orpington. That this color problem is a serious one, the following remarks on "Mating for Color in Blacks," by E. Campbell in his book "The Orpington and Its Varieties," London, England, 1902, prove:

"In Blacks there are three general faults to be guarded against:—

"Firstly, a dull brown feather which, however it has been produced, is rightly condemned by every judge, no matter how big the bird that carries it. It is possible to use pullets of this sort if they have sufficient merit in size, type, and bone to warrant it; but since they require extra bright green cockerels, with sound blue-black under-color and fluff—birds difficult to get—or in more experimental breeder's hands a red-hackled or saddle-splashed cockerel, since these invariably throw good colored pullets, they are seldom worth persevering with.

"The next, and more general fault, is a dull black that seems to carry no sheen on the pullets and to bring a bronze lustre on the cockerel's tail. A bird so handicapped must carry great size and type to beat a better colored bird.

"The last—some would put it first—is the objectionable blue or purple Minorca sheen with which some of our best typed and biggest birds have been exhibited. This blue does not often extend beyond the back, breast, and wing-bow but sometimes it shows even in the tail coverts and sickles. It is almost as difficult to breed out as the brown tinge, but although it is equally contrary to the Standard, I, and very many others, do not (because it gives the bird a more brilliant appearance) class it so objectionable as the brown or lack lustre blacks.

"I am inclined to think that blueness is a result of too much color, that is to say, of breeding too much for high sheen. I think it arose and arises from using red-hackled males in the breeding pens without discrimination. Why I think it a result of excess in color is that I have noticed a blue cockerel who runs out in a bright sun for some time, loses much of the blue color where the sun has got at the feathers, while underneath, and where the feathers have overlapped, the blueness remains. Similarly, when such a bird is well shaded the blue often loses its vividness in a subdued purple—which is an excess of blue. The sun appears to draw out the blue to some extent, just as it would extract the brightness of a buff or dim the most vivid green.

"A blue pullet—though not a cockerel—often moults into a good green hen, but all the same, blue is a great fault in color and is at times difficult to breed out. If you examine a Black Orpington's feather, say from the wing-bow, in a strong light, you will find that each feather consists of traversing and alternating bars of yellowish, rich purple, green and bronze green lustres. These vary in vividness and intensity with the general color of the bird. If the bird appears blue in plumage the purple bar will dominate the others and often run down the shaft as well. If the bird has a dull green color the bars are nearly equal in strength, but their sheen is subdued. If it has a real satiny green sheen the green bar will dominate and the

bronze green will be absent, the purple dwindling away to a mere line.

"It is by studying the various strengths of these bars that I hold you can best improve the color of your birds. The laws of color tell you that the infusion of red into green and blue will turn green into blue and blue into purple. I have never met anybody who has gone into this matter or even noticed this peculiar barring in Blacks, and I have gone into it here with an idea of showing that it accounts for the difficulty one sometimes encounters in improving color. It is obvious that the fact that these sheens or lustres lie in distinct bars makes it necessary to broaden or intensify the green bar only if we want good color. Now, most black breeders know that the greenest of pullets throw red-hackled or saddled cockerels, and are thrown by them. That fact has led the indiscriminating breeder to assume that a red-hackled cockerel is the proper mating to secure the highest green sheen. But, as I have pointed out, the excessive use of a bird of this description usually ends in a blue or purple cockerel being evolved, and pullets which lose their vivid green to assume a purplish black.

"The worst point about the use of a red-splashed cock is that the pullets very seldom indicate it save in their brilliant color, and, it may be, in a narrow line of feathers at the root of the comb. As it is possible to breed equally brilliant pullets without using a red-splashed bird, the unknowing will purchase a hen of this red cockerel character only to find that the money has been largely thrown away, for the resulting cockerels seldom fail to show red in hackle or saddle.

"There are two ways of getting rid of the objectionable purple. One is to breed back to the green, the other to overpower the purple by a sound satiny green which has been secured by true breeding and not infusions of red. The most satisfactory is the latter, but since one must needs know the antecedents of the stock used, it is most difficult at times to adopt it.

"To breed back I would simply procure a cock of the preceding generation of the same strain and in which the blue had not appeared. Failing this I would get a cockerel on whose feather the purple and blue bars were as indistinct as possible, even tolerating a sad colored bird for the sake of the correction, since the result would probably be brighter colored chickens than the cock and better colored ones than their mothers.

"But the shortest road is undoubtedly through a deep vivid satiny green cock, in whose feather no trace shows of either blue, purple or red. The overpowering nature of this bird's color is such that the yellow bar is narrowed and the green widened until the blue is almost swamped or pushed farther into the purple.

"There is no use mating up blue and bronze birds or blue and brown birds. These require that brilliant green that I have just written of. To improve merely sad colored birds you may use a red-hackled cockerel if you are content to throw away all the resulting cockerels. It will be cheaper at the start than mating up a good green bird, but in the end it may not. If you have a good blue cockerel which you must go on with, give him green or dull pullets."

FIRST PRIZE BLACK ORP'T'N HEN CHICAGO DEC. 1908.
BRED AND OWNED BY
G. E. GREENWOOD   LAKE MILLS WIS.

Economic Qualities of Black Orpingtons

Professor Edward Brown in his latest Standard work, "Races of Domestic Poultry," London, England, in re-

FIRST, SECOND AND THIRD PRIZE COCK'LS, BOSTON, 1910. OWEN FARMS, VINEYARD HAVEN, MASS., U.S.A.

FIRST, SECOND AND THIRD PRIZE PULLETS, BOSTON, 1910. OWEN FARMS, VINEYARD HAVEN, MASS., U.S.A.

viewing the economic qualities of Black Orpingtons, remarks:

"The Black Orpington is a big, bulky fowl; hardy, but not very rapid in growth, as it is somewhat heavy in bone. It carries a fair amount of flesh, which is greyish-white in color, but is fine and delicate in skin. There is too much flesh upon the legs to regard it as a first-class table fowl, though that flesh is juicy and decidedly superior to what is found upon more active fowls. The bird fattens fairly well, but its grey flesh detracts from its appearance when dead. The breast meat is not very abundant, considering the size of body. The hens are good layers, especially in winter, and the eggs are medium in size and in tint. For general purposes, and especially for birds which must be kept in confinement, in towns and manufacturing districts, its black plumage is a great recommendation. All varieties of Orpingtons are good sitters and mothers."

The views of prominent American breeders of Black Orpingtons on breeding for exhibition and market are expressed in the following articles contributed by them to this chapter.

Breeding for Color and Shape

Feeding Does Not Influence Color—Correct Type in Both Male and Female Not Necessary to Produce Best Results

G. E. Greenwood

MY experience with the Black Orpington dates back to the year 1904, when I imported a trio of birds. In this short time there has been a wonderful change in the type of the Black Orpington, especially in the American bred birds. Nearly all of the imported birds are very large and of good color, but are too high up on legs to suit the American breeder. The type that is winning at our largest shows is the low down massive type, and to produce birds of this type, you must breed from both male and female with these characteristics. Do not expect to strike a happy medium by using low down females and a male bird up on legs. It requires patience and a great amount of skill to produce a flock of birds of uniform type. Another point of vital importance in breeding good Black Orpingtons, is breast shape. Never use a male or female in your matings with a flat breast; it is not Orpington type. An ideal Black Orpington has short, stout legs, broad back, deep body, full round breast, short, well spread tail, black eyes, and a beautiful beetle green color. Such birds are hard to get, but by close culling, and breeding from the best each year you are bound to get a few good ones. Color seems to be the stumbling block of all Black Orpington breeders, although in the past year several birds were shown at New York, Boston, and Chicago, that were nearly perfect in color. Having bred Minorcas a great many years I was well qualified to help in perfecting the color of the Black Orpington.

In selecting the male for the breeding pen be sure he has a rich, black under-color, a male with light under-color is sure to produce poor color in his offspring. I have often seen the statement that two highly colored birds mated together would produce birds showing purple barring. Now, how in the world are we going to get birds of good color, if we do not use in our mating birds of the best color obtainable. To get rid of this plum color you must use birds, both male and female, as nearly perfect in color as you can get them. From such a mating you may expect a good percentage of finely colored birds.

Feeding Does Not Influence Color

I do not believe feeding has anything to do with the color of Black Orpingtons. I have experimented along this line for a number of years, and have found the only way to get good color is to breed it by proper mating. Avoid using a male bird with white in flight feathers, especially in both wings. I have used a bird in my matings with white in one wing without serious trouble. The better way is to cull out all birds showing white in any part of the plumage, because when once bred into your flock it is hard to eradicate. The Black Orpington is truly a grand fowl and is becoming more popular each year. In fact, it is destined to become the most popular black fowl on earth. I have bred Plymouth Rocks, White Wyandottes, Black Minorcas, and White Leghorns in the past twelve years, and I can truthfully say that the Black Orpington is the best winter layer, and the best table fowl of them all.

Value as Utility Fowl

The points of utility which make a breed of most value to farmers and small breeders are egg production, good size, hardiness, good sitters and mothers, and a good table fowl. In all these the Black Orpingtons have been tried and not found wanting. They are a full breasted, heavy quartered bird, both valuable characteristics in a table fowl, and they also possess that other quality, a white skin, so desirable in that it indicates tenderness of flesh, both in broilers and in full grown birds. The Black Orpington can justly be termed the best all purpose fowl in existence. They are making rapid progress in America, and have behind them one of the best specialty clubs devoted to the breed, composed of true fanciers and business men, who will see that the Black Orpington is placed at the head of the procession, where it justly belongs.

Merits of the Black Orpingtons

Breed True to Type—Great Layers—Superb Table Fowl —Hardy, Quick Maturing, Quiet Disposition

D. N. Foster

AFTER twenty years it can be truly said that Black Orpingtons breed perfectly true to type and color, and the veriest amateur can produce as fine Black Orpingtons for the show pen as the most expert.

This is proved over and over again in England, where a beginner at the shows frequently takes the prize away from the old fancier. The Black Orpingtons have a lovely gloss on their plumage, of a beautiful beetle-green shade.

Their faces and combs are a rich red; they have dark eyes, the darker the better; in the best birds they are almost black.

They lay brown shelled eggs and their flesh is light colored.

The cocks weigh ten to twelve pounds and the hens from eight to ten pounds. The plumage should be close and not loose, the skin thin and fine in texture, and flesh firm.

Quick Maturity

No heavy all-purpose fowl matures so quickly. The pullets begin laying when about five months of age and the cockerels when well fed and cared for, weigh a pound for every month of their age, up to nine or ten months. As early broilers they cannot be excelled.

"LADY RUTH"

Second Prize Hen, Indianapolis, Indiana, 1910. Bred and owned by Blue Ribbon Poultry Farm, Columbus, Ind.

Hardiness

I have no other variety so vigorous and healthy. A sick Orpington is a novelty in the chicken yard.

The "Duke of Kent," at this writing five years old, is as active as a cockerel of ten months.

Meat

The Black Orpington is the greatest table fowl ever

produced. The skin is white, thin and tender, not yellow, thick and tough, and so greasy that children will not eat it.

Like the markets across the ocean, the best American markets are already demanding a white skin fowl, and the day is not far distant when its greater desirability will be generally understood.

The Orpingtons are especially noted for their deep bodies and broad, full breasts, the long breast bone carrying almost as much white meat as is found upon a turkey.

Eggs

They are wonderful layers of large, smooth, brown eggs. Pullets hatched in April and May commence laying in early winter, when eggs are most desired, and will keep up laying until spring, if warmly housed and fed green cut bone and green food, after winter sets in. In the celebrated Australian contest in egg laying, where all breeds competed, a Black Orpington pen headed the list, the second being a pen of Silver Wyandottes and the third a pen of White Leghorns.

Out of forty-one pens, the Orpingtons held seven of the highest thirteen places.

Plumage

The plumage is most attractive, excelling the Langshan in that beautiful green sheen, for which it is so greatly admired. Makers of hat trimmings and ladies' boas, are today offering 20 cents an ounce, ($3.20 per pound) for the neck, saddle and tail feathers, and from 14 cents to 18 cents an ounce for the best of the feathers from some other parts of the body. Dust, smoke and coal dust does not show upon their plumage, making them a particularly pretty fowl for town life.

Disposition

They are quiet and peaceful, do not fly, and bear confinement well. They are easily kept from sitting, but when desired make good sitters and mothers.

Easily Bred

They breed truer to color and type than any other variety, and frequently from high-class fowls or eggs, hardly a single cull bird will be found. They are, therefore, especially adapted to the beginner.

Shape and Size

Black Orpingtons Immense in Size, with Characteristic Shape Possessed by No Other Breed

M. F. Delano

TO MOST PEOPLE there is no handsomer sight than a flock of big black fowl running around on a nice green lawn, with their bright, brilliant green sheen, red combs and wattles, and their beady black eyes. As long as the writer remembers the leading black varieties have been rightly termed a gentleman's fowl. As I understand this term it means a grand, all-around fowl that is a fine table fowl, a splendid layer and of unsurpassed beauty, but which for some reason is handicapped from a utility standpoint. For many years the Black Langshan enjoyed great popularity. In fact in the early nineties it enjoyed a remarkable boom, the writer being among the breeders to take it up at that time, and a more satisfactory fowl for home use was never produced than was the Langshan of the early nineties.

The Black Orpington is made up largely from Langshan ancestors. With the Langshan was combined the blood of the Cochin, the Minorca and other varieties, all yielding together the desirable points of each, and the Black Orpington today is far and away the finest black fowl that has even been produced. The old expression, "As lordly as a Langshan," can be applied with even greater force to the Black Orpington of today. Their immense size, profuse feathering and attractive type combine to make them "The fowl of beauty and a joy forever." The Black Orpington was the first Orpington produced and they were the product of skillful scientific breeding in an effort to produce an all-around utility fowl of greater value than any then in existence and the originators were certainly successful in getting what they were after.

In England, where the Orpington was originated, a white or pink skin commands the highest market price in both poultry and ducks. They prefer it there to a yellow skin. In this country we have always been partial to yellow skinned fowls, but today the tremendous merit of the Orpington as a table fowl has broken down the barrier of prejudice and they are commanding the top prices in the best markets where a really fine table fowl is most highly appreciated.

The Blacks are the cobbiest and lowest down of all the Orpington family. This effect is brought about to a very great extent by the abundance and looseness of the feathering which they inherit from their Cochin ancestors. They have a type that is very distinctively their own and I do not believe that the other varieties of Orpingtons will be brought to this type without seriously impairing them as utility fowls. They are of tremendous size and average very large, fully developed cock birds, often weighing fourteen and fifteen pounds, and hens ten and eleven pounds. They are very long, extremely deep from the back to the hock, and have great breadth. Not only do they show this effect while living, but the carcass has the same characteristic and they have an abundance of delicious breast meat on their well-rounded breast that is of quality that will delight the epicure.

As I said above, the beauty of outline of the Black Orpington is helped greatly by the profusion and length of the feathers. This is true of every part of the bird. The male has an abundance of saddle hangers and tail coverts which cover a fairly long main tail. There is not an angle of any kind in a really good shaped Black and their lines are drawn with the length and breadth of the Plymouth Rock and Brahma and the curves of the Wyandotte. A truly attractive bird that is rapidly gaining a high place in the public favor, that stands today as the most popular black fowl that has even been produced and that has the intrinsic merit to hold the place which it has won and to gain new friends and admirers every year. Every lover of a black fowl should take up the Orpington and I have never known a case yet where they have not given absolute satisfaction. As a table fowl, as layers of large brown eggs, and as an adornment to any place, they are without a peer.

English Black Orpingtons

Selecting, Mating and Breeding for Type, Size and Color to Produce the Massive Black Orpingtons of England

W. M. Bell

ORIGINATED some twenty years ago, the Black Orpington has maintained a steady popularity as an exhibition fowl. The reason of this is not far to seek, for it is first, a very handsome bird, second, easy to prepare for exhibition, and third, no double mating is required, equally good birds of either sex being produced from the same pen. The late Mr. W. Cook, who originated the breed, is stated to have used a cross between a Minorca cock and black sports from Plymouth Rocks, mating the progeny back to clean-legged Langshan cockerels. However, this may be, the result has been a short-legged, deep-bodied bird with brilliant sheen and broad, full front.

Taking the three main characteristics to aim for in the breeding of Black Orpingtons as shortness of leg, color, and, most important of all, type. I will first speak as to shortness of leg. Occasionally we see birds penned, that almost touch the ground, so short are they, and, although we want short-legged birds, this is rather overstretching the mark. Being full-bodied fowls, they must have a certain amount of day-light under them to show off the full effect of their body type. Birds that are as short in leg as I speak of very seldom attain a good size, and an Orpington must have size. The color should be brilliant beetle-green sheen, free from purple or bronze and one of the chief aims in breeding is to get this color not only on the top, but carried right down the breast into the fluff. At the present time there are very few birds that can show a really good color throughout. In type they should have a broad, full front, showing an unbroken curve from the beak to the tail. Many birds have a tendency towards being pinched in the breast, and one of the main objects is to get this perfect curve. The body should be deep through, as it is no use having a broad, full-fronted bird if it has not the depth of body to set it

BLACK ORPINGTON COCK—LATE ENGLISH TYPE

Reproduced from "Races of Domestic Fowls," page 54. Bird was bred by W. M. Bell, England. He has exhibited with success in America, winning recently at Madison Square Garden, New York and at Boston. Mr. Bell accompanied his exhibit and made numerous friends on this side of the Atlantic.

off. The back should be short, with broad shoulders, with the saddle rising in a gentle sweep up to a neat, flowing tail. The saddle itself should be broad, with a full hackle. The comb should be fine, evenly serrated, and free from side sprigs. It should be medium size, set on a firm base. If too small, it makes the cock look effeminate; but, on the other hand, a comb like a Minorca's tends to lessen the compact appearances of the bird.

The eye is an important point and its color is sometimes the subject of controversy. I have often heard people talking of a jet black eye, but have never seen one yet. However good a bird's eye may be, if held in the light it will show a dark brown iris with black center.

In the mating of Black Orpingtons I am never particular as to the size of the male. In fact I would prefer a small bird, if he is of really typical shape. The female should be as large as possible, provided she is a fairly good type and other small points are good. In both cases they should have good bone and should stand on short legs, this applying more especially to the male. Never mate two very highly colored birds together, as by doing so one is liable to get purple barring on the wing, or a bronze color, either of which goes against a bird in the show pen.

I have mentioned double mating as not being necessary for this variety. For the amateur who only keeps one pen this is a great consideration. I have known a case of a cockerel winning at the Dairy Show and a pullet getting second on the same day both birds being hatched on the same day and bred from the same father and mother.

In conclusion, the perfect bird has not been produced yet, but should this happy consumation of the breeders' wish be obtained, it will be difficult for any man to produce a more perfect picture of the feathered tribe than a Black Orpington.—Illustrated Poultry Record, England.

CHAPTER IV

Buff Orpingtons

Severe Criticisms and Condemnation of the New Variety when First Exhibited in England—Rapid Growth in Popularity of Buff Orpingtons when Their Good Qualities Became Better Known—Mating for Size, Type and Color—Contributions by Noted American Breeders of Buff Orpingtons

J. H. Drevenstedt

BUFF Orpingtons followed closely on the heels of their black namesake, but even with no claim as blood relations, they shared the growing popularity of the Orpington fowl in England with the Blacks from the start, while in this country they became the most popular variety from the time they were first exhibited at the Madison Square Garden in 1899 and continued in the lead up till the present time, although the White variety has come along with a rush in the past few years, and bids fair to overtake its Buff rival, as it already has its Black in number of entries at our leading poultry exhibitions. But Buff color is so immensely popular with American fanciers that any variety of a breed possessing it, is bound to remain among the leading races of domestic poultry, provided it meets the necessary other requirements which make up the much sought after, but rarely found general purpose fowl.

The new Buff Orpingtons were launched upon a stormy sea and were tossed about roughly in their youthful days. The originator, William Cook, was severely criticised and even roundly abused in his native land, for offering an imperfect cross-bred fowl to the public, as well as for his temerity in calling these Buff crosses "Orpingtons" when no trace of the original Black Orpington blood flowed in the new comers' veins.

The American Fancier in the fall of 1901 published several caustic comments by the late Harrison Weir, one of England's most noted and respected poultry authorities, which handled Mr. Cook's Orpington productions without gloves. Capt. C. W. Gedney, Bromley, Kent, England, in the October 27th issue of the American Fancier contributed another severe criticism of Buff Orpingtons, which in part read as follows:

"I read with much delight the well merited castigation administered by Mr. Harrison Weir to William Cook, the Orpington poultry dealer. But it will make no impression upon this Barnum of the English poultry world. I hope, however, that it will counteract some of the log rolling of W. Cook, which has been so long rampant in the American poultry journals. The English people—at least some of them—like being gulled, and W. Cook apparently found this out in 1883. He has gulled them successfully ever since and waxed fat upon the proceeds.

But to get to one of his latest mongrels—the Buff Orpington. I induced a friend of mine at a distance to obtain for me a sitting of these birds' eggs from W. Cook direct. There were eight chickens hatched from the 13 eggs, but two of them were white! Seven out of the eight had perfect Dorking feet, with five toes, and six of the brood were feather legged! Such a lovely lot of mongrels! And this does not exhaust the list of 'Orpington' varieties which I got for my money. Two of the Buff chickens are now in adult plumage and they are distinctly marked upon their backs with dark lacings, suggestive of Plymouth Rocks! The feathering on the legs is very slight and it has a tendency to disappear as the bird gets older. At any rate, I was told so by one of W. Cook's representatives. He did not, however, explain, as Mr. Harrison Weir does, that the feathers are to be pulled out and the holes filled up with wax! As I said before, the British public like being gulled, and they took William Cook's mongrel Black Orpington in preference to the pure Langshan, because he boomed it and lied about it wholesale."

ENGLISH BUFF ORPINGTONS, 1906.
Reproduced from Races of Domestic Poultry, by Edward Brown, England.

No doubt, Captain Gedney was somewhat prejudiced in favor of his Langshans, which, added to his neighborly feelings toward Mr. Cook, may have caused the above severe condemnation. Our English cousins when they attack each other in print, do not hesitate to call a "spade a spade," or refrain from personalities. But every man has his friends, so Mr. Cook was not left alone to fight his battles, as the following letter, in answer to Mr. Gedney's, which appeared in the January 12th, 1902, issue of the American Fancier, will prove:

"As a breeder and admirer of the Orpington, I have read with much interest the correspondence that has recently appeared in the American Fancier regarding the Buff variety. Mr. C. W. Gedney's letter in your issue of 27th of October was evidently dictated by a spirit of personal animosity towards Mr. Cook, who, I am sure, from personal knowledge of him, does not merit the severe and wholesale condemnation passed upon him by Mr. Gedney. Surely the English public must be very stupid indeed if they have allowed themselves to be 'gulled' for 17 years, and we in the Australian Colonies must be equally stupid, for as each new variety of Orpingtons is introduced at home it is very soon thereafter imported here and eagerly welcomed. I think Mr. Gedney must have drawn largely upon his imagination in his description of the chicks hatched from the sitting of Buffs he refers to, for I have hatched scores of sittings during the past three years and have never had or heard of anything approaching such results. Mr. Cook, instead of attempting to conceal, has frankly told both verbally and in writing the composition of the Orpington fowls, and so those persons who breed Buffs are neither surprised nor disappointed when some of the chicks are not a true buff color or have a few feathers in their legs. My own experience has been that the chickens are very free from feathers on the legs and only a very small percentage have specks in the body feathers. Admitting that such flaws occur occasionally, these are only regarded at all seriously by exhibitors and in no way detract from the value of the Buffs as utility fowls of the highest standard. In this Colony the Orpingtons are bred in large numbers, being held in high estimation on account of their superiority as early and prolific layers and as quick maturing table birds. The government poultry expert here stated in a recent report that the Orpingtons were by a long way the best breed of utility fowl ever imported into this Colony. On that account alone are the praises bestowed upon them not well merited and may not the deprecatory remarks about the breed and the personal abuse of their clever creator be treated with contempt? The Diamond Jubilee Orpingtons recently imported here have already proved their immense value as utility fowls and, like the others, have come to stay. I would only add that in my opinion, Mr. Cook has deservedly earned the warmest gratitude of poultry keepers in this Colony as elsewhere for having produced a breed of fowls which is second to none, if not superior to all others, for utility purposes, and are moreover wholly undeserving of the name of 'mongrels' which Mr. Gedney applies to them.   E. BUTCHER.
"Sydney, New South Wales."

The above correspondence appeared at a time when Buff Orpingtons began to gain a foothold in America. In 1901 at the New York Show, Buff Orpingtons were out in great force and showed high quality, according to the reports at that time. Such well known fanciers as F. W. Gaylor, Chas. Bennington, Chas. Vass and S. D. Furminger became interested in breeding Buff Orpingtons, and as it fell to our lot to judge Orpington classes in those days we could readily note the rapid advance made in comparatively few years in the color and combs of the English importations and in the American bred specimens. But type was still far removed from what the Standard called for. The birds were leggy and lacked breadth and depth of body. In 1902 the Orpington fever took firm hold of American breeders, as the following report of the Orpingtons at the New York Show of that year written by the enthusiastic Orpington champion, Wallace P. Willett, indicates.

At the New York Show in 1902 there were 63 Orpington birds shown by eleven breeders against 23 by five breeders last year. This shows how rapidly this breed is coming into favor, making its own way quietly and without any pushing thus far. The breeders exhibiting this year were C. E. Vass, Washington, N. J., Frank W. Gaylor, Newport, R. I., Wallace P. Willett, East Orange, N. J., P. Kyle, Flushing, L. I., Chas. Edw. Faber, Plainfield, N. J., Arthur J. McCain, Delaware, N. J., H. M. Carpenter, Ossining, N. Y., Jas. S. Warne, Washington, N. J., Edmont Poultry Farm, New Milford, N. Y., and Mrs. J. G. Osborne, Fabius, N. Y.

"The first on Buff cock went to Mrs. Osborne; 1st hen and cockerel to C. E. Vass; 1st Buff pullet to Mr. Gaylor; 1st Black male and female to Mr. Carpenter; 1st Buff pen to Mr. Willett. Mr. Willett exhibited the Spangled and Jubilee varieties as well as the Buffs and Blacks. Next year Secretary Crawford promises special classes for Buff, Black, Jubilee, and Spangled, Wm. Cook & Sons,

COCKEREL IN FIRST PRIZE PEN. BOSTON JAN 1910.
BRED AND OWNED BY OWEN FARMS, VINEYARD HAVEN, MASS. U.S.A.

the originators of the Orpingtons having agreed to see all classes filled. Mr. Wm. Cook, Senior, had made arrangements to be present this year with four pens but was prevented by sickness.

"The American Orpington Club held its first annual meeting and elected Mr. C. E. Vass, president; Mr. Frank W. Gaylor, vice-president; Mr. Wallace P. Willett, secretary and treasurer; Mr. P. Kyle and Mr. C. E. Faber, members of executive committee. Standards were adopted for all the varieties. A new paper appeared called 'The Orpington,' by Wallace P. Willett, devoted entirely to the interest of the breeders of the fashionable, fancy and utility of Orpingtons, 1-cent stamp for copy. This paper gives the English Standards of all the Orpingtons and a fine illustration of a typical Black Orpington cock. The wonderful progress made by the Orpingtons in England and the Colonies in the few years since their introduction is only a forerunner of what will come about in the United States."

In 1903 came the floodtide boom of the Buff Orpingtons, when William Cook arrived from England with a ship-load of Orpingtons of all varieties and made such a display of them at the Madison Square Garden. That exhibit firmly and permanently established Buff Orpingtons, as well as the Black and White varieties in America. The boom was on in full blast, and has shown no signs of "blowing up." Buff Orpingtons are here to stay.

Buff Orpingtons in England

The late Lewis Wright in his "Book of Poultry" relates the history of the first appearance of Buff Orpingtons in England as follows:

"The first pair of Buff Orpingtons ever shown as such were exhibited by Mr. W. Cook, at the Dairy Show, October, 1894, when Mr. Cook drew our especial attention to them, and made the same statement which has been made on many other occasions, that they were produced by mating a Golden-spangled Hamburg with a colored Dorking hen, pullets from the produce being mated with a Buff Cochin cock; the main characteristic of the birds being the combination of buff plumage with white legs and feet. We remarked on this earliest possible occasion, that a fowl with such points might probably prove both valuable and popular; but that there was grave objection to calling them Orpingtons, since he had already appropriated that name to another fowl, which had, according to his own account, not one single element in common. He asserted, as he has done since, his right to

FIRST PRIZE WINNING HEN BOSTON 1910.
OWEN FARMS, VINEYARD HAVEN, MASS.

call any fowl he introduced by any name he pleased; to which we replied in substance, as expressed more definitely later, that a breeder might justifiably use 'any name he likes really open to him; but when a man has already appropriated the name of his own residence to one such breed, of which he tells us the components were A, B, and C, there are the gravest objections to his giving, years afterwards, the same name, for merely trade and advertising purposes, to another 'breed,' which, according to his own account, has no particle of A, B, and C, but was built up of X, Y, and Z.' Such nomenclature would not have been allowed by the Poultry Association of America, and objection to it was widely expressed by the most prominent authorities in England with scarcely an exception; the already existing Orpington Club also protested against the same name being given to another fowl which had not in it one atom of the same constituent as theirs. A considerable amount of discussion took place later emphasized by the fact that precisely similar fowls were exhibited under another name at the Smithfield Show of dead poultry. Owing largely to this latter circumstance, the question was finally brought before the Poultry Club, who decided that it was then too late to interfere, but intimated that such a case would not again be allowed to pass unnoticed; and in this way it is to be hoped that the circumstances may have produced a more definite understanding concerning such matters in the poultry world."

Of the subsequent development of Buff Orpingtons by English breeders Mr. Wright writes as follows:

"There is an abundance of evidence that all breeders who took up the new breed found plenty of work to do in it, and that some of them selected simply the best specimens they could find, wherever they could find them, in Surrey or Lincolnshire, or anywhere. That birds have been bought in the latter county of people who have bred nothing else for a quarter of a century, were shown directly as Buff Orpingtons, and used by Buff Orpington breeders, is quite certain; and various successful strains have no doubt had different local origins which accounts for the fact stated by Mr. Richardson presently, of the evil results found to follow from crossing these different strains. None of the early show specimens had the shape of the Black Orpington, all being higher on the leg, longer in the back, and less massive in the body; but breeders have recently been paying more attention to weight and shape, which are accordingly improving.

"The merits and utility of the breed stand apart from its origin and name. Those who objected to the latter, were accused of making a 'virulent attack upon the breed,' but without, as far as we know, any foundation. The fowl itself was recognized by nearly all as a most valuable one, endorsed already by the long experience of the Lincolnshire breeders as a first-class breed for the market; and speedily found, as soon as kept alive for other purposes than market, to be a most hardy bird and prolific layer. Putting aside claims and proceedings to which there are serious reasons for taking exception, Mr. Cook may be given full credit for 'booming' and making known in other than poultry-fattening circles, what is recognized as one of the most attractive and useful of all classes of poultry, combining the beautiful and popular buff color, with admirable table and laying qualities. It is probable that the Buff Orpington, as now known, comes as near to the ideal of an all-round, general purpose fowl as is humanly possible; and it is not a small service, however we may regret the methods employed, to have made such a bird popular amongst breeders generally."

Buff Orpingtons Admitted to the Standard in 1903

Single Comb Buff Orpingtons were admitted to the American Standard of Perfection of 1903, but the 1905 edition of the Standard contains the first revised ideal shape illustrations of Orpingtons, the color description being the same in both. No material change is made in the description of buff color in the revised Standard of 1910, but changes in shape were made by the Revision Committee at Chicago, Ill., April, 1909. These changes will be found in the "Comparison of Type Columns" of Chapter II. of this book.

WINNER OF FIRST PULLET BOSTON 1909 AND NATIONAL S.C. BUFF ORPINGTON CLUB SPECIAL FOR BEST PULLET. OWNED AND EXHIBITED BY HENRY B. PRESCOTT, VILLAGE STATION, DERRY, N.H.

Buff Color

The Standard color for all American Buff fowls is defined as a rich golden buff, free from shafting or mealiness, the surface of the head, neck, back, wing-bows, saddle sickles being of a rich golden sheen in the male; the same surface color predominating in the female, the glossy lustre on the surface harmonizing in shade with it in all sections. Under-color is a lighter shade of buff, which must be free from foreign color, while black or gray appearing in wings or tail is a serious defect. A first-class specimen is of one even shade of color from top of head to tip of tail over back and wings and around breast and body. This is the ideal American Standard buff color, hard to attain, but the true guide for the breeder, one that has been instrumental in producing magnificent specimens of Buff Cochins, Buff Wyandottes, Buff Plymouth Rocks, Buff Leghorns and Buff Orpingtons in America. There is no flexibility in this Standard color ideal, for it means that only true buff color can win, other points being equal in exhibition specimens. English breeders are less strenuous and considerate over this buff color section than American fanciers as the following definition from the English Standard for Buff Orpingtons will show:

"Plumage: Any shade of buff from lemon buff to rich buff, on the one side avoiding washiness, and on the other side a reddish tinge. The color to be perfectly uniform throughout, allowing for greater lustre on the hackle and saddle feathers, and of the wing-bow in the case of the cock only."

This will explain the variation in color of imported Buff Orpingtons which frequently disappoints American purchasers. But English breeders are great sticklers for type, and size and color take a back seat when a corking good big and shapely Buff Orpington makes his appearance. But it is a very good law in breeding all kinds of feathered live stock to get shape or type first and color afterward.

Size and Weight

Orpingtons are large fowls, so that size without corresponding weight is apt to kill the type and the breed. That is the chief reason why many Buff Orpington breeders objected to a reduction in the Standard weights of Orpingtons, and justly so. A comparison of weights in England and America shows:

English	American
Cock:—Between 9 and 10 lbs when fully matured.	10
Hen:—About 7 or 8 lbs. when fully matured.	8
Cockerel:—Not given	8½
Pullet:—Not given	7

So on the weight question the English and American Orpington Standard agree.

Disqualifications

The English Standard "passes" Buff Orpingtons for the following: "Serious Defects; other than four toes; wry tail or any deformity; the slightest feather or fluff on legs or feet; long legs; yellow skin; twist or side spikes to comb or comb over to one side; yellow legs or feet; any white or much black in tail or flights; legs any color but white." The American Standard of Perfection gives the following color disqualification: "Positive white in ear-lobes covering more than one-third of the surface; yellow beak or skin; shanks other than white or pinkish white." Other disqualifications for deformities come under the head of "General Disqualifications;" which are nearly the same as in the English Standard except that no mention is made in the American Orpington Standard of the number of toes an Orpington is required to have on each foot, although it is generally understood that five-toed specimens are to be disqualified by the judges.

The excellent articles on Mating, Breeding and Rearing Buff Orpingtons contributed to this chapter by foremost American breeders which follow should prove of great value to all lovers of this popular and useful variety.

Mating Buff Orpingtons

Proper Selection of Breeders to Overcome Defects in the Buff Orpingtons—Extremes of Color in Mating are to be Avoided

Maurice F. Delano

EVERY true fancier is a member of a large family which includes the men whose bread and butter depend on their ability to produce the highest excellence; the men who breed pure-bred poultry as a side issue, but also as a means of augmenting their incomes, and the men who breed thoroughbreds for recreation or for the love of it, but to whom the commercial success or failure of their hobby is not of particular moment. At heart these cousins of differing personalities are very similar, and they are equally fascinated in watching the chicks shape up, and can hardly take their eyes from the specimens that promise to land the laurel wreaths at the coming shows. No class of fanciers in the world are abler men, better sportsmen, or have a harder color to produce in its perfection, than those devoting their energies to perfection of buff color in the various breeds.

Considering its hybrid origin, the Buff Orpington has made wonderful advancement, and the best specimens average fully as good in color as do the Buff Rocks and the Buff Wyandottes. These latter varieties were originated just a little earlier, but had much less alien blood of absolutely foreign color that must be eliminated to produce the soft even buff color so coveted by all breeders of buff fowls.

The Buff Orpington of today breeds remarkably true to both type and color and the percentage of decided culls is but little larger from flocks bred from properly mated pens than it is in flocks of the older buff breeds. A few more years of careful selection will put them on a par from a fancy stand-point with any of their sister varieties.

The commonest shape faults in the variety as we find it today are; a little too much length of shank; breast not quite full enough, and keel not quite level enough for true Orpington type, which should be long and broad as well as deep, in fact a low down bird of tremendous frame. A tail carried too high will shorten the apparent length of a bird, and the majority of males show this defect to a more or less degree. Great strides are being made every year in correcting these shape or type faults and the progress made is most encouraging.

The list of color defects will take longer to eradicate, but this is true of any variety in existence. If it were possible to produce birds approaching perfection in a majority of our flocks, our interest in the science of breeding would cease. White showing in under-color of hackle, in wings, and at base of tail is a fault it will take many years to completely rectify and not lose our richness and evenness of surface color. Minor color defects that are fast disappearing are: red wing-bows in males;

FIRST PRIZE BUFF ORPINGTON PULLET
MADISON SQUARE GARDEN N.Y. 1909-10.
DUNROBIN FARM   CHATHAM N.J.

penciling or ticking in females; bluish legs, a trace of their Hamburg ancestors; and mealiness and patchiness in both sexes. Other defects that will be a little troublesome for some time are stubs on legs, and yellow shanks showing Cochin blood; side sprigs on comb, and white in ear-lobe, two more reminders of the Hamburg blood. The writer has seen but one specimen showing the fifth toe of the Dorking, so that possible defect can be ignored.

The above list of defects appears quite formidable but is no more so than can be written of any variety if we tabulate all the faults appearing in the poorest specimens raised. In the proper mating of any flock of poultry we should strive first to produce the breed type, second, to improve the color of plumage; and third, to perfect the minor points such as comb, eye, lobe, and legs. I will take them up in this order.

Breed Type Emphasized

Too much stress cannot be laid on the importance of breed type in any variety. A poorly shaped Orpington can approach the Plymouth Rock, the Wyandotte, or worse yet, the original Hamburg in type. This last is getting rare and of the other two, the first is least objectionable. Select a male as good in type as you possess that is not really bad in other desirable sections; and mate with him the best colored hens you have that are up to, or over Standard weight. If your male is poor in comb, be careful to have hens as good in this section as possible. (Do not, however, sacrifice shape and size to comb. Our American taste demands a low Plymouth Rock comb on our Orpingtons and this is not natural to the breed. It will require patience to produce good combs without sacrificing size.) Such a mating will produce large boned birds that have size and type in a goodly percentage. If the chicks lose in color, this weakness can be rectified in succeeding matings. As a rule the male will influence the color and type more than the female does, while the latter influences the size. For this reason I would prefer a smallish male of really good type to a tall gawky male having nothing but size and color to recommend him.

Among the first principles of color mating there are a few points I wish to make most emphatic. Never, under any circumstances, use extremes of color. Never use a female in your best pens showing mealiness over the wing-bows. Never use a reddish female with the web of the feather very pronounced, or as we say, "shafty." Never use a male with a red hackle, and, at the same time white in under-color of hackle. Good buff color was never produced by using birds indicated above, excepting in an occasional chance specimen.

How to Obtain Color

In mating for color, I first select the best colored males I have available that have no bad outs in other sections. These birds I line up, and carefully compare their breeding possibilities from a color stand-point, taking the known qualities of their direct ancestors into consideration. After selecting the most promising bird, I go through our flock of females and select even colored birds ranging from the same shade as the male to two tones darker. I make color the first consideration in selecting these females, but also carefully weigh their breeding, and choose only those that have the proper blood lines to nick with the male, and that are strong in the sections where he is weakest. This insures improvement all along the line. This process is repeated with each one of my selected males; in each case using females that are not over two tones away from the male in color. The light-er males are mated with females that are absolutely sound in under-color in every section. It is not necessary to mate dark females with such a bird, as the lighter females that are sound under will have the necessary strength of color pigment to mate with a male whose origin is known. The darker males are usually very sound in under-color, yet the same rule applies, and females mated with them are even and rich in color, with sound under-color. In all selected females, I avoid absolutely all mealiness and shafting when possible. Also give the preference to hens that have moulted right, and to pullets that my experience has taught me will make fine hens.

Extreme matings containing dark birds of one sex and light birds of the other will never produce medium shades. The result will be unattractive patchy pullets with dark hackles, and uneven cockerels with dark hackles

"CHAMPION" NEW YORKER

First prize Buff Orpington Cock at Madison Square Garden, New York, 1909-10; also winner of cup for "Best Orpington Male, all Varieties." Owned and bred by H. H. Kingston, Jr.

and wing-bows. Cockerels from an extreme mating usually average slightly better quality than do pullets. The contrary is true of a proper mating as it is easier to produce sound colored pullets in quantities than it is to produce sound males.

In correcting comb and eye defects I am careful in every mating I make, whether primarily for shape, or for color, to have good eyes and comb on either male or females. When possible, I avoid a decidedly bad comb in either sex. I do not believe it practicable just now to discard an otherwise fine male for a large, or unevenly serrated comb. This section will adjust itself with time and should not be allowed undue prominence. We all admire a five point comb that is perfectly serrated, but the longer we breed our favorites the more this section seems to diminish in relative importance. Never breed from a bird having side sprigs, or from one having stubs on shanks.

Leg color runs very good in the breed. A small percentage still show bluish shanks, and a still smaller number come with bright yellow legs. Simply do not breed from these birds no matter how good they are in other sections. Bright red eyes on birds of extra good color are not plentiful. Have made decided progress this year in this section, and a few years will largely do away with our greenish, yellow, and fish eyes. As I said before, if you use a male with poor eyes, rectify the defect in your females, and vice versa. There are a fery few fanciers of any breed that do not admire a buff bird of the true golden shade, and of even color. The writer has bred over twenty varieties since he began eighteen years ago, and the buffs have always been first in his affection. My long experience in breeding Buff Rocks and Buff Wyandottes is extremely valuable in producing proper color on the Orpingtons. Today, I am completely cured of my prejudice against the white legs and skin of the Orpington and can watch our Orpington and Rock chicks running side by side with equal pleasure. It is a keen delight to note the improvement in both varieties, and it is still an open question which will produce the best colored bird this year. That the Orpington stands a chance in such a competition shows decided improvement, and we have cockerels and pullets of both varieties without a trace of foreign color in wing or tail.

The Buff variety has proven itself to be the best of the Orpingtons, and has firmly established itself as one of the six most popular varieties in America. Its intrinsic merit will retain it in the proud position it has attained, and probably place it near the top of the leading six. It is a fowl for the fancier, the egg farmer, and, as the popular prejudice against the white skin and legs disappears it will be a very popular fowl for the broiler and the capon man.

Some Experiences with Buff Orpingtons

Why I Selected the Buffs and How I Started— Success in the Show Room

Miss Henrietta E. Hooker

MY first experience with poultry began about ten years ago as a necessity or rather economy, in disposing of table waste from a large family. They were a mongrel collection of twelve, purchased at auction for 48c each. A cousin of mine, a fancier of Buff Rocks, approved my venture, but urged that I keep something in fowls that my relatives would not be ashamed of as they neared my house, and generously proposed if I would eat what I had, to start me with six good Buffs.

This proposition was accepted and my flock was soon all buff.

A Matter of Sentiment

In company with a friend of mine I made a walking tour in England a few years ago and was so charmed with the region about the little town of Orpington, that when after my return home I began to see Orpington fowls mentioned in the poultry papers, without knowing anything further about them than what the name suggested, I decided to own some—for there is something in a name.

A Start

I sent to a man in the Middle States who advertised imported stock for a sitting of eggs, paying what seemed to me then the enormous price of five dollars for twelve eggs. These eggs were put with eggs from my own flock under two hens and though the Rock eggs all gave me chicks, not an Orpington peeped. On opening the eggs, only one chick, a monstrosity, was to be found. In reply to my report the shipper said he had broken up his breeding pens but would sell me chicks cheap in the fall. This, followed up, brought the report that his brooders had burned, leaving him no surplus for sale. Thus vanished my first five dollars.

When the first eggs failed I wrote to a New Hampshire breeder advertising for three dollars a sitting and soon had eggs going with the same result as the first. The sender said that I must in some way be at fault but I could have another sitting at half price which I took, getting therefrom a cockerel and a pullet, the former with fully feathered shanks, the latter with as much white as buff and about equally distributed and my labors for that season ended by finding that the pullet laid well and the cockerel was fine eating.

About this time I chanced to see in a poultry paper the question answered as to whether it was practicable to import eggs, the reply being that the writer knew of seventeen Buff Orpington chicks hatched from two imported sittings. Here was my opportunity and I importuned the writer to secure for me a pair of these chicks. The importer, it proved, was not a dealer and hesitated to spare a pullet as nine were cockerels, but finally sold me a pair, five months old, for $6.00.

They were from the yards of the originator, Mr. Wm. Cook, and were duly named William and Lady Gladstone.

I bought a hen from a well known breeder for $3.00 and felt that I was on my feet; but the hen died two weeks later and the eggs from my pair did not hatch. Perhaps I should not expect it now from a six months old pair with no others in the pen.

I knew nothing of "points" at that time, only what the papers mentioned in descriptions, but I am sure that the pullet I should today consider choice and also that "William" had some white flight feathers.

Some people might have been discouraged. Some might have had other feelings. But for years the motto in my laboratory had been: "Keeping everlastingly at it brings success," and in this spirit I determined to persevere until I had Orpingtons.

Soon, however, the eggs from my pair began to produce results and I was encouraged. A year later Mr. Cook, Senior, came from England with 103 birds.

"PERTELOTE"
First Prize Hen New York, 1908. Owned by Miss Henrietta E. Hooker.

One of these, a cockerel, I purchased and mated with a part of my pullets, bringing reasonably good results.

I had no thought of exhibiting birds until a year or two later. Indeed, I am sure that my attitude toward what used to be called "hen shows" has materially changed or I should not now show birds.

Making Headway

After a little I needed new blood, I was told. I purchased a cockerel for $15.00 at a Connecticut show and felt that I had gone beyond all limits of extravagance. I ascertained that this cockerel was sired by the first New York cock in 1903. This bird was beautiful as he developed and I declined an offer of fifty dollars for him. He sired the hen which I still own and which has always won when shown. She is the mother of my hen, "Pertelote," who won first at New York in 1908, and of many good hens in my flock.

I have made many mistakes but have tried to learn from every available source. In my early mating I had expert advice and also in preparing my first birds for showing. It was money well invested. I visited, when possible, the poultry plants of others, both of this country and England, and learned always something helpful.

Introducing New Blood

New blood is introduced with extreme caution and carefully toemarked more than one year. I have disposed of every chick from such mating because of undesirable qualities thus introduced.

I have three times imported cockerels from England;

BUFF ORPINGTON COCK
Winner of first prize and cup at Allentown, Pa., 1908; first, two silver cups and gold special for best shaped male at Madison Square Garden, New York, 1908-9; first and shape special at Boston, 1909, and first at Cleveland, 1909. Bred and owned by Sunswick Poultry Farm.

twice direct from the home estate of Mr. Wm. Cook, Sr., and once from Mr. Wm. Bell. I have never paid what would be considered high prices as I could not afford it and most of the work of my small poultry plant I do myself.

My First Exhibition

My first experience in showing birds was at Springfield, Mass., and was on this wise: A family of college girls in my home noticed that at the coming poultry show a five pound box of chocolate creams was offered to the woman whose exhibit won the most points and begged me to send my hens down to secure the creams for them; as a joke I promised to do it.

I knew nothing of shows, had visited but one, but I had a slight acquaintance with Mr. Frank Gaylor, and induced him to come and teach me how to select and prepare birds for showing. He was very generous and to his help I owe more than to any other outside assistance my success in selecting and showing birds.

Won the Chocolates and Cup

Perhaps no mortal was ever more amazed than I was at the outcome of this show. Not only did I take the chocolate creams but the cup and many specials. Since then I have never failed to win a fair share of the trophies whenever my birds have shown and the same may be said of my stock.

Demand for Quality Increases Each Year

At the close of the season I have about fifty hens and raise about 150 chicks, this being the capacity of my village lot. I find there is always a market at proper prices for first-class stock and could have sold much more this year could I have spared it. It is very noticeable that the demand for first quality in stock and eggs increases each year. In offering eggs this year at $3, $5 and $10 per sitting, hardly anyone wished the two lower grades. I have no pens especially mated for myself from which I do not sell and I also hatch eggs for myself from each mated pen.

No Secret Methods—Hard Work—Study

I spend much of my time with my fowls and know them as individuals. I have no secret methods but find that success comes only from good, hard work and plenty of it; careful attention to little things, all the time; cleanliness; good food; fresh air and gentle treatment. These make strong, quiet birds, easy to deal with. I am very fond of my flock (especially so of individuals) for which I care almost entirely myself. This has been a restful diversion from my life-long work of teaching. I find the Orpingtons very domestic, generous the year round to my egg basket, especially good as a table fowl, beautiful to look at and very hardy.

They Will Sit

They are far from being non-sitters, but easily broken if taken in season, gentle when sitting and the best of mothers.

As they lay all winter they are ready as early as one wishes to set eggs, even in January or February.

I believe if we are conscientious in culling for the next few years and careful in mating we have the foundation of the most beautiful breed of fowls as well as the most useful that any country can produce.

A Good All-Around Fowl

As broilers they are sooner ready for market than any I have tried, so we have in the Orpington an all-around fowl, considered from the standpoint of meat, eggs or early broilers, and certainly the soft tint of golden buff in chick or older fowl is a joy to the eye.

Ambitious

I have an ambition, perhaps selfish, one day to raise as good Orpingtons as are to be had. I am slowly, carefully and with great enthusiasm working toward it, failing oftener than I succeed but learning what not to do next time and expectant of better results each year.

Buff Orpington Type and Color

H. H. Kingston, Jr.

SUCCESS in breeding Buff Orpingtons, like success in any undertaking, is the result of careful thought, diligent application and hard work, though all three are a pleasure when combined with a business or a hobby we enjoy. There is money in breeding good Buff Orpingtons, but don't think you can step into success all at once. I repeat. it takes thought, application and work, and I might add—time, to build up a paying business.

The Golden Rule in breeding Buffs is:—The male transmits type and color; the female transmits size. Follow this rule carefully and you will succeed. Like all good rules, it has exceptions. Here is the important one; do not breed males and females widely different in color. A golden buff male mated to dark females will never produce exhibition specimens.

Let us step out in the poultry yards and mate up our next year's pens. We will first collect all our well matured males and make our selections from them. Here is a fine looking fellow with fine shape but red on the wing bows and almost white under-color. He is no good—never could breed good color from such a specimen: put him in the fattening pen. Well, here is another, of beautiful even color and nice type, but look at that side sprig on his comb. We hate to do it, but out he goes.

Thus we cull them over till there are a select few left. These have good type, even surface color, though some are a few shades darker than others, good under-color, clear buff wings, short, stocky, pink shanks, good head, comb and eye. The darkest fellows will show some black in the main tail feathers but none have white in any section. We pick out the very best one, band him and enter his band number in our stock record book under pen number one, band 19 and so on down the list with the others.

Next we judge over the hens and pullets, always late in the fall or winter after the hens have fully moulted. First, we sort out all the largest hens which have moulted out a rich even buff, taking it for granted that these have been culled over for defects when pullets. We select the best for mating with our best cockerel and record them in the book under his pen.

Now we come to the pullets. First, pick out the largest, then cull them over for defects. Throw out all birds that show any trace of mealiness or shafting and then select the pullets that have a good even surface color of rich golden hue, neat, small combs, red eyes, short, heavy shanks and good, deep bodies. Mate these with the best cock we have picked out that is a shade or two lighter and we have pen number two.

In all matings aim to compensate the defects of one sex by good points in the same section of the other. Furthermore, do not mate a lot of nondescript females to one male and expect to get good chicks on the hit-and-miss principle for it will usually be miss. If you haven't enough females to mate up a full pen, use two or three of the very best and you will be rewarded in the fall by a lot of youngsters that will make your heart glad.

I have learned through costly experience that the shortest road to success in breeding Buffs, is to buy stock from one reliable breeder, whose birds have been winning consistently for a number of years. After getting such stock, stick to it, and when you need fresh blood, go to that same breeder for it.

By way of closing my advice is that you will make no mistake in taking up Buff Orpingtons. As a breed they are the most popular breed of buff fowls and will always remain so. Their many good characteristics are told on other pages herein by abler pens than mine.

Why We Breed Buff Orpingtons

J. M. Williams and Co.

WHEN the question is asked, why do we breed Orpingtons, Rocks, Wyandottes, or in fact any breed, for a profit, the breeder of his particular variety believes that he has the best birds for making money, either for the fancy or common purposes, and will be backed up by scores of other breeders. This we not only find in the poultry business, but in every vocation in life. To make a success of any business we must like it—believe in it, and love to do the work connected with it; then with the proper push necessary in any business and the faculty of letting the people know what you have to sell, you have the main secret of success in any business.

We like the Orpington family from start to finish, not only because we have made a financial success of it, but for the many good qualities they possess. In our several years breeding them we have become so attached to them that they seem like one of the family. The general characteristics or make-up of the Orpingtons is such as to make it easily understood, but they have taken a prominent place among the old breeds in so short a time and will continue to hold it for all time, not only for a general purpose fowl, but in the fancy as well.

While we breed and keep the Buff, and White, in both Single and Rose Comb varieties, we must admit that the Single Comb Buff is our choice beyond any question, and is, we believe, the most prominent today in the poultry fraternity, still, there are lots of friends in the other colors and we will not take issue with them on that score, as we keep them and like them well.

In taking the Orpingtons for a general purpose fowl

WINNERS AT MADISON SQUARE GARDEN, NEW YORK, 1908-09. FIRST COCKEREL AND SECOND PULLET
J. M. WILLIAMS AND CO., BREEDER AND OWNERS.   NORTH ADAMS, MICHIGAN, U.S.A.

WINNERS OF FIRST PRIZE ON PEN, NEW YORK DEC 27-1909-JAN-1-1910
OWEN FARMS.   VINEYARD HAVEN, MASS., U.S.A.

we want to consider all the points essential to the make-up of any general purpose fowl, and we know that the Orpingtons will land in the front ranks. We claim early maturity, egg production, hardy constitution and table qualities second to none. Under early maturity we have with proper care and feed produced pullets laying at four and one-half months of age, but allowing five months as the average will compare favorably with any breed, and as to the production we refer to the many tests by experimental stations, who are disinterested parties, and which is the only fair test, and we always find the Orpingtons leading or in the very first ranks.

We farm out a good many birds and we hear the same story from nearly every one: how much better the Orpingtons lay than our own birds. While this pleases us still we know that our competitors in other breeds will say that anyone can get that kind of a testimonial. Anyway, it pleases us.

We do not feed for winter layers, breeding for fancy, as we would if for common market purposes, as we are every year over-sold on our egg orders for early chicks; so we commence to feed for our egg sales in February; still we have more than we can use in the early winter months, just feeding some of the coarse feeds, not intended for feed layers.

In table qualities the Dorking blood used in the make-up of the Orpingtons is one of England's greatest table fowls; the plump bodies of the fine texture of meat is not only of the finest quality but of sufficient quantity to satisfy anyone in that direction.

We find the Orpingtons of a very hardy constitution, and one of the most active of the largest breeds of fowls, the young, middle-age or matured fowls are the same in this respect—they are working from early morning until late at night. We believe in letting them hustle at nature's way to find at least a part of their living; this not only lessens the expense, but we think we get results in this way provided by nature, that is much better than any artificial food that is used as a substitute. We find our young birds growing from the start and always show the picture of a healthy condition in this way of handling young or old stock.

The Orpingtons are a cold weather bird, as you might say, that is, they stand the cold winters and are not pinched up as a lot of our small variety birds are. They seem to have a winter's dress adapted to that purpose and stand the cold weather better than some of our people.

The beauty of the Orpingtons is second to none from the fancier's standpoint, with that deep, broad, massive body so characteristic in the Orpington family, with a golden buff, or a green sheen, or a pure white, whichever color your choice is, is certainly a picture in itself. We do not care what breed you are breeding or admire, when you stop and look at a pen of Orpingtons as bred today by our leading Orpington breeders you cannot help but admire them. In the show room you will always see someone admiring them, whether a breeder or not.

Some seven years ago when we took up the Orpingtons, you could count the breeders on your fingers; now there are thousands breeding them. In every state in the Union, in the show room, we find the entries challenging the old breeds of Rocks and Wyandottes, and we look for the time in the near future when they will head the list in our big shows of New York, Boston and Chicago.

How We Raise Buff Orpingtons

W. H. Bushell

THE Buff Orpington has come to stay. Why? Because they do not disappoint and they come up to all that has been said about them by the introducers, the importers and the American breeders in general.

They are a grand all-around fowl.

When we say that their meat is tender, juicy and of fine flavor, we mean just that. All chickens might be tender, but there is a difference in flavor and some are more juicy than others.

As a winter layer they are the equal of the best.

The farmers are beginning to realize their value as an all-around fowl, and as a winter layer, especially, so the demand for male birds from farmers with which to improve their flocks, is great.

They are also buying lots of eggs for hatching, and thus putting thorough-bred Orpingtons onto their farms.

Many of our farmer friends and acquaintances tell us that the Orpingtons are the best bird they ever raised for layers, and their heavy weight and fine meat make them very popular and profitable, when they get ready to turn them into cash.

Another feature that takes well with the farmer is the fact that they are such great foragers. They make nice quiet sitters, easy to handle and make good mothers.

The chicks are hardy and easy to raise. They feather out rather slowly but that is to their advantage. A chick that feathers out too fast uses the most of its vitality to make feathers instead of bodily growth, consequently they are very susceptible to the many chick ills, and easily succumb.

We find in our own experience that artificial methods are by far the best for hatching and brooding. We have used the high-grade incubators for the last twelve or fifteen years, have done all of our hatching with them, and have raised the chicks in brooders.

We prefer a 100 chick capacity brooder for 50 chicks. Lamp brooders are used in our brooder house, which is 12x70 feet. It is a frame building with drop siding on the outside and lined on the inside with brick. The brick is laid on edge between the 2x4 studding, and in this way leaves a one inch air space between siding and brick.

The building is divided by one-inch mesh wire partitions, into pens three feet wide. A hot-water furnace furnishes the heat through two one-inch pipes, which run the length of the building on the north side. It keeps the temperature from 50 to 60 degrees in winter.

We feed a patent chick feed and some hard boiled eggs chopped fine, for the first three weeks, and then add rolled oats to their rations. A few sods of blue grass are in each pen for them to pick at. Rolled oats, or pin-head oats are great bone and muscle builders. As long as these youngsters are confined in the runs, we keep the yards spaded up and keep coal ashes, sand and blue grass sods in them, and we are never bothered with bowel trouble.

After the chicks are six weeks old, they are given free range and are fed as follows:—

In the morning they get a mash composed of coarse cornmeal and rolled oat meal, equal parts, that has been soaked over night in cold skim milk. For dinner they are given boiled potatoes, carrots and beets. For supper, whole wheat; wheat bran is kept before them all the time, but they are never given more than they will eat up clean, of the other rations.

Our laying stock never gets any corn except on very cold, winter days; then they are given corn at night. Wheat screenings are the main feed in winter. We give them alfalfa leaves to scratch in, no other green food and no mashes. Eggs run very fertile and hatch good strong chicks. We use the stoneware drinking fountains, which are emptied every night in winter. They are filled every morning with warm water.

Our matings consist of 7 or 8 hens with one male bird, in the winter time, in a pen 8x20 feet. They do not go out of the house sometimes for a month or more at a time, especially if the weather is cold and snow on the ground. The yards are 100x200 feet, are seeded with blue grass and also contain plenty of fruit trees for shade.

The chickens never get the best of the blue grass. Some of the yards were sown to blue grass twenty years ago and it is still very thick. During the breeding season we take the male birds away from their mates every night and put them in a separate pen and give each one all the corn he will eat, and put him back with his mates in the morning.

With these methods we not only enjoy the work but have had good success in raising the best breed of all, The Buff Orpington.

CHAPTER V

White Orpingtons

Rapid Rise in Popularity and Remarkable Boom of the Variety in America—Shrewd Business Methods of Promoters—Improvement in Color, Size and Type—Breeding and Feeding for Color and Character

J. H. Drevenstedt

"PEGGY"

The Sensational Hen That Made White Orpingtons Famous and Popular in America

FIVE years ago, White Orpingtons were trailing behind the Buffs and Blacks; today they are being trailed by the latter, so great has been the increase in their popularity, not only in this country, but in England as well. This sudden boom of the White Orpington was not entirely due to the surpassing merit or beauty of the new variety itself, but due to the shrewdness and ability of Ernest Kellerstrass in advertising and pushing it to the front. Mr. Kellerstrass, like other breeders of White Orpingtons, was impressed with their intrinsic value as layers and for market fowl as well as their attractiveness as a large and beautiful exhibition fowl. But unlike others he believed in telling the poultry raisers of the United States all about these good qualities in a way unheard of in the history of poultry culture of America. Just before he started on his campaign of advertising the White Orpington, we happened to be at a noted fancier's yards, and after looking over his favorite Barred Plymouth Rocks, we came across a fine pen of White Orpingtons. "What are you doing with those Orpingtons?" we inquired. "Nothing," he replied and added: "I never had a breed of fowl I liked better than these White Orpingtons; they breed well, are hardy and the hens are splendid layers in winter, excelling other breeds in this respect, and no better table fowl can be asked for. But nobody wants White Orpingtons, so I am going to sell them the first chance I get." Shortly after that he disposed of the entire flock at three dollars a head. The following year, 1907, Mr. Kellerstrass sent a few White Orpingtons to the Jamestown Exposition among the lot being the now world-famous "Peggy," a White Orpington hen of some merit, in fact she was the class of the Orpington exhibit, shape, size and color being almost perfectly blended in this sensational and most widely advertised chicken in the world. "Peggy" became an attraction at leading fall fairs and winter shows, being advertised and exhibited in true showman's style, press and advance agents creating curiosity and widespread in-

terest among visitors. There was a rush to see "Peggy" wherever she was exhibited, the crowds being greater at the Southern State Fairs held at Nashville, Memphis and Atlanta, thanks to the clever newspaper notices which appeared in the daily papers. The gold leg band presented to "Peggy," the golden cage decorated with choice flowers and a dozen other little wrinkles illustrating the great value of "Peggy, the 10,000 dollar hen" all conspired to make White Orpingtons the most talked of fowls in America.

Then came the great Paderewski sale, by which Mr. Kellerstrass transferred a very fine pen of White Orpingtons to Madam Paderewski and the latter transferred 7,500 dollars in Uncle Sam's yellowbacks to Kellerstrass' bank account. This was the largest price ever received for a pen of chickens and will stand as a record for years to come.

This was followed by a boom in White Orpingtons, such as has never been equalled by any other variety of poultry in the past. The man who gave up White Orpingtons because nobody cared for them, had a good thing but did not know how to push it. It's the men behind the breed that make or break it.

W. H. Cook in "The Orpington and Its Varieties," London, England, 1908, writes:

"One of the most handsome and profitable varieties of the Orpington family is certainly the White. Introduced in the year 1903, they have grown in popular favor ever since, simply on their merits as a perfect all-round fowl, and whether used for utility or exhibition purposes, or in hot or cold climates, the same report is heard,— they thrive splendidly, are most popular, and there is always a ready sale wherever they are introduced.

"Their origin is somewhat remarkable, as, in the first place, the originator, in breeding the Buff Orpington, was surprised to find many chickens coming pure white, and as these sports grew, their color remained absolutely snow white; they appeared to be thicker set or more cobby specimens than the then existing Buffs, and by experimenting in mating these sports (which by the way were all pullets) to White Cochin, White Dorking, and

REPRESENTATIVE ENGLISH WHITE ORPINGTON MALES
Reproduced From "Feathered World," London, England

White Game male birds, the White Orpington was produced, and is today perhaps the most popular variety of the Orpingtons. It might be advisable to here add that occasionally a single specimen will revert to one of the above named male birds used in their production, therefore one may see a little feather on the leg from the Cochin, a fifth toe from the Dorking or a tinge of yellow in the legs, feet, and beak. These defects are now rarely seen on stock bred from the best and most reliable strains.

"There is one great advantage to purchasers, and that is double mating is not required, as equally good cockerels and pullets are bred from the same pen, and this alone has greatly assisted the variety to become so popular in almost every part of the globe. As layers of large, rich colored brown eggs they have no equal, commencing at five to six months old, laying throughout the winter and spring. They possess sterling qualities as a table fowl, being quick growers, short on leg, long and full in breast, and are ready for killing quite twenty-four to thirty days before other pure breeds. Heavy clay soil has no drawbacks for them, and as a general all-around fowl for the cottager, farmer, or fancier, they are today unequalled.

Hundreds of White Orpington male birds are used annually for crossing purposes, as among a mixed lot of hens, even if mongrels, the progeny grow faster, and the pullets are better layers than with any other mating; therefore, as a general all-around utility fowl, they are now known the world over as the finest and best.

"As an exhibition fowl they are most popular, the classes provided for them always being well filled, and the average visitor to a show will remark upon their handsome appearance and symmetrical outline. Even the best are not hard to breed, as, provided the birds are well bred and kept growing from birth, no difficulty will be experienced in rearing specimens to the highest standard by even amateurs or those who are practically inexperienced in the raising of high class fowls."

The above is a fair and comprehensive presentation of the virtues and faults of the White Orpington from an English point of view. Few American breeders of White Orpingtons will file any objections to the above optimistic and eulogistic opinions expressed by the son of the originator of these immensely popular white fowls. Neither is there any serious difference of opinion existing between

REPRESENTATIVE ENGLISH WHITE ORPINGTON FEMALES
Reproduced From "Feathered World," London, England

American and English fanciers in regard to the type, size and color of White Orpingtons as good breeders in both countries are striving toward the same ideal in shape and size.

The Kellerstrass harvest was such a bountiful one that other shrewd fanciers became interested in White Orpingtons so that classes at our leading shows began to swell to large proportions. Such noted exhibitors as Owen Farms, Sunswick Farm, William Cook & Sons, Lawrence Jackson and others dividing the honors with the Kellerstrass entries. At the New York and Baltimore Shows of 1910, one hundred and thirty-four White Orpingtons were exhibited at the former and one hundred and twenty-seven at the latter, exceeding the Buffs in numbers at Baltimore by twenty-three specimens and coming within the same number of equaling the Buffs at New York. This indicated the present status of the breed in the East, although at the Boston show the Whites ranked third to Buffs first and the Blacks second for the past three years. In the West and South, the Buffs still have a formidable lead, the race for second place being a close one between the Blacks and the Whites, with the latter slightly in the lead. A study of the tables pre-pared by D. E. Hale showing the relative popularity of the different varieties of Orpingtons at leading exhibitions, which appear in the later chapter of this book, will prove interesting and pleasing to lovers of White Orpingtons.

Improvement in Shape

In shape the White Orpington has progressed rapidly, rivaling the Blacks in this respect, but not reaching the size and weight of the latter as a rule. They also show less softness and profusion of body and fluff feathering and more length of shank than the Blacks, which in the opinion of conservative breeders is a very good fault. There seems to be a tendency among some breeders toward a more Cochiny bodied type, which is more readily noticeable in the females illustrated by artists on the other side of the Atlantic. We reprint on page 27 an illustration of a pair of White Orpingtons from "The Orpington and Its Varieties," Feathered World, England, 1909, which shows the large and rather loose feathered and low hanging body, fluff, departing from the "U" shaped body line and the original cobby type of Orpingtons. The male retains this "U" shaped body line and cobby look.

White Orpingtons in England

The boom of the White Orpington in the United States has traveled across the seas reaching England several years ago and it looks as if English fanciers have been caught in the boom most completely. White Orpingtons are certainly booming in England; judging by the following remarks of R. H. Davis in "Poultry," England: "Whites, which are going ahead by leaps and bounds, and bid fair to become the most popular variety of the day since they are capital layers and table birds, can be thoroughly recommended as a good investment. One of the highest prices (if not the highest), namely $375, was paid for a White Orpington Cock last year (1909)." The illustrations of noted winners at the Crystal Palace Show in 1909, which we reprint from the "Feathered World," on pages 48 and 49, convey an excellent idea of the type and size of English White Orpingtons, showing the great improvement made in this direction by the breeders on the other side. As our English cousins are very proud of white-legged and white skinned poultry and like plenty of "beef" or size in utilitarian breeds, the White Orpington ought to become the most popular all around fowl in England.

White Plumage Hereditary

Color is due to hereditary sources, the excess or absence of one of the primary colors that are found in domesticated races of poultry influencing the strength or weakness of the various shades produced. Black and red are the two pigments that play an important part in determining the shade of buff and white. The excess of one over the other influences the plumage of white fowls. Where red is the strongest the white is apt to be creamy in the under-color and brassy on the surface; when black is the strongest, we are apt

A TYPICAL ORPINGTON HEN

to get the whitest birds, i. e. of that snow white or silvery tinge so popular among fanciers of white fowl. This is easily noticeable in chicks when first hatched showing gray backs, and in matured cockerels and pullets showing gray ticking. Such birds have silvery white quills and if selected as breeders will reproduce the same color, regardless of the color of the grain fed. On the other hand matured specimens with creamy plumage and yellow quills will not be made to produce silvery white plumage and quills by feeding white grains only. The hereditary tendency of the red pigment is there and can only be bred out by careful selection and mating of the whitest breeders each year, or by using a black out cross. Some strains of White Wyandottes, White Plymouth Rocks and White Leghorns rarely produce anything but silvery white progeny, notwithstanding the fact that their owners have fed yellow corn year after year. Neither has climate any effect on such silvery white birds, as we have seen just as fine ones raised in the Sunny South as in the colder northern, eastern and western states, where Old Sol is only in his glory for a few months of the summer. It is true that exposure to the sun and rain in summer and fall will often cause brassy hackles, backs, wing-bows and saddles in old males, but as a rule where the silvery white blood is strongest the brassiness is absent regardless of exposure to sun and rain.

Handling and Feeding for Exhibition

There are, however, many good breeders who firmly believe that the color of the grain fed affects the color of the plumage of white fowls, and their views are entitled to considerable respect and demand careful consideration. One of the best articles on this subject appeared

A NOTED WHITE ORPINGTON WINNER

twenty years ago in an English poultry journal. It was written by an old experienced breeder and exhibitor who practiced what he preached and believed in his methods of feeding and preparing white fowl for exhibition.

After dwelling on the importance and necessity of natural shade and grass runs in the summer months for growing stock, he describes in detail the methods of raising white poultry in confined runs as follows:—

"But, supposing that shade cannot be procured naturally, then we must seek for it artificially, as undoubtedly white birds enclosed in yards or grass runs without trees should have it. We have known artichokes, sunflowers, dahlias, even stinging nettles and coarse docks, make admirable shelter from the sun, for we are convinced that whenever possible shade should be living shade. Were we to keep one growing white cockerel in a run planted with artichokes, and a duplicate in a run of the same size, walled in, and roofed in by iron or wood, or even calico, then we should readily see in two months' time which would be the victor.

"When the chickens are three months old we like to have them placed in such shade as can be got, and there kept. Two runs (we are writing now for those who can not give their birds their liberty) side by side, as large as can be spared, are very suitable for a flock of white cockerels or pullets. In the one have the dahlias or artichokes, or such like (which, we need not mention, must have a certain growth before the chickens are turned in, or the plants will be trampled down and become worthless), and let the other be one-half short grass and one-half arable, the latter being dug over once a week. The chickens can then be shifted from run to run by drawing up a slide between them, according to the state of the weather or season. When these herbaceous plants have died down the sun will have, to a great extent, lost its power, and the birds may then be left more exposed.

"We have known, too, a troop of White Cochin pullets do grandly in a well-earthed potato plot, getting both shade and insect food. White Dorkings or Leghorns would, however, do too much damage to the tubers to allow of their being turned in. Again, when the artichokes or sunflowers, etc., cannot be got, the next best substitute that we know of is to plant the runs with boughs of spruce fir. These soon turn brown, we know, but they

A PULLET OF GREAT SIZE

hold their spines a long time and really afford capital shade. When the birds have got their growth, then sheds with wire fronts or covered in with newly invented wire-woven roofing gauze can be used, and the birds, with plenty of good food, should do well, but while they are growing, until they attain their matured plumage, we cannot too strongly advise that their runs should be airy and sheltered from the sun's rays by a living growth of vegetation.

"Thus much for the chickens. Now let us turn to the moulting out of white poultry. We like the hens to sit in June or July. Sometimes we let them sit on dummy eggs for four or five weeks and then turn them down in a good grass run. At another we give them half a dozen eggs to hatch if they like—not for the chickens they may rear so much as for the rest it will afford the mothers. Hens so treated moult out quickly and early; their feathers all come off together and not in patches, and the new plumage grows quickly, the feathers coming strong and firm. These birds should not, however, have a cock running with them until they are taken to the breeding pen. Cocks should be put in small warm runs in July with plenty of dust and road grit. They, too, will then moult out early and well—far better than if they had their liberty. Care only must be taken to see that they feed heartily, for occasionally they seem at first to pine for their freedom if they have been accustomed to it and get below par when their moulting out becomes tedious and the new plumage patchy. Green food, especially lettuces, we like to see given ungrudgingly, and sods of grass cut two or three inches thick are much appreciated, which when done with and allowed to dry make excellent mould for potting flowers or material for dust baths.

"Many think that white poultry can be easily moulted, that their feathers are bound to come white and that the process is consequently an easy one, but this is far from the truth of the case, for as much care and attention is wanted to get a white bird through its moult as ever is needed for a colored one and perhaps more, for while slight stains or tinges would not show probably in the

WHITE ORPINGTON COCK—AMERICAN TYPE

latter, in the former they glare out conspicuously in contrast to the rest of the white plumage.

"Before concluding this subject we would take the opportunity of saying that neither maize nor Indian meal should be given to white poultry. Birds fed for any length of time on such food will, in all probability, become creamy in plumage and lose that spotless whiteness which is so greatly desirable. We are aware that some of the samples of Indian corn are much whiter in husk and substance than are others, but with good wheat, buckwheat and dari, maize of no description need form any part of the daily food of white exhibition fowls."

The statement in the last paragraph above relating to the feeding or rather to the not feeding of yellow corn, will be received by many breeders with doubt as to its correctness, no experiments having been made to determine what effect, if any, the feeding of yellow corn to fowl has on the shade of white plumage from which correct conclusions can be formed. It is true that a number of prominent American breeders of White Leghorns and White Plymouth Rocks believe that yellow corn causes creaminess and brassiness of white plumage when fed daily to young and old fowls, even when fed only as a part of the grain ration. These breeders feed white corn in place of the yellow, being convinced that it will at least prevent the appearance of the yellow tinge in the feathers of naturally white birds, even if it will not whiten the plumage of specimens that have a yellow streak in their make-up.

Size and Character

In order to increase the size and weight of White Orpingtons some English breeders have resorted to crossing the latter with the Blacks. The veteran fancier and Judge J. W. Ludlow in the "Feathered World," England, of September 2, 1910, comments on such crosses as follows:

"Bye-the-bye, blacks being the safest occasional cross for the produce of bulky whites, it will become necessary to carefully examine and guard against grizzly under fluff in all and any of the black progeny thus produced. An occasional dip is good, over much leads to spoil the glossy splendor and produce a dull black plumage. In fact, the advantage is to the whites only to the detriment of the blacks so crossed. I name this because I know that, in the effort to get size, bulk and character in whites, some of the biggest blacks have been and are used for the purpose."

We are of the opinion that the infusion of Black Orpington blood into the Whites has also had a beneficial effect on the white plumage, eliminating the tendency to brassiness in the males and creaminess in the females. Recent importations of White Orpingtons possessed this desirable silvery white plumage in a more marked degree than in the earlier Whites received from England, the Black no doubt being responsible for both size and color improvement.

The Story of The White Orpington

How and Why, After Many Years of Experimenting with Various Breeds, the White Orpington was Selected as the Best Fowl for All Purposes.

Ernest Kellerstrass

AN IDEAL WHITE ORPINGTON

YOU ask me why I selected the White Orpington. Well, no doubt you are aware of the fact that I have bred chickens for many years and I bred something like sixteen or seventeen different varieties, and the great trouble was some of the birds that I had did not produce the eggs. Then I bred some other varieties that produced the eggs, but they were too small and would not produce the meat. I looked around and experimented for a number of years, and after I had tried out some Orpingtons for about three years under lock and key here, I finally came to the conclusion that they were the birds. I got rid of everything on the farm and went to breeding White Orpingtons exclusively.

With due respect to all other breeders and other breeds of birds, I think there is nothing like the White Orpingtons. History shows that they mature quicker than any other breed of fowl. It is no trouble to find White Orpingtons laying at four or four and a half months old, but those are common occurrences. Then again, for the meat end of it, the birds have to weigh a pound more than any other breed, according to the American Standard, that is in the clean-legged variety and as to producing the eggs,

FIRST COCKEREL KANSAS CITY SHOW 1910
— — — BRED AND OWNED BY W.R. KENDALL.
605 NEW NELSON BLDG., KANSAS CITY, MO. — — —

take them in any breeder's hands or in the hands of our experimental stations, and look through the poultry journals and size them up and you will find that they are as good if not better than any other known breed, when it comes to egg producing.

There is only one thing that I would like to guard all breeders against, and that is be careful when breeding for show purposes. Some of the best breeds in this country have been ruined by people just trying to breed for feathers, and forgetting the utility end of it.

Now my main object is just to try and see how good egg producers and how large fowls I can produce. It is eggs and meat I am after. Take the commercial end of it away from a breed and it will soon fall by the way-side. It does not matter how good your birds are in the showroom, nor how many ribbons they will take, if they do not produce the eggs and meat, they will soon lose in popularity. Every day I am writing to my various customers telling them especially when it comes along about mating time to be very careful in selecting their birds and not breed them for feathers alone, but to always remember the most important part is just meat and eggs. Of course lots of people say today that the White Orpingtons are now on a wonderful boom. I think that is wrong; there is no wonderful boom. There is simply a demand. The farmers and the breeders and the city fellow and all of us want meat and eggs, and the Orpingtons produce those two things,

and that is the reason why everybody wants them.

There is going to be a steady demand for the White Orpington for years and years to come. They are a fowl that is here to stay and to stay just as long as they will "deliver the goods," not forgetting the commercial end of it; just as soon as they do that, the White Orpington, like a good many other breeds, will fall by the wayside.

White Orpingtons Best Layers

Comparison of the Three Varieties as Utility Fowl

E. A. Haring

IN THE beginning I wish to say that I realize that some strains or families of fowls are better than others of the same breed, having seen this proved time and again.

There has been so much written as to the origin of the Orpington that I will not attempt to go into that. I was first attracted to them by seeing a photo of Whites in a poultry paper, and made up my mind that they were the coming breed. I bought a few pullets from one of the foremost breeders and a sitting of eggs from another from which to establish a strain of my own.

From the time those pullets started to lay, they outlaid any stock I had ever handled. Afterwards, in taking charge of one of the largest and best flocks of Orpingtons in this country, I found the same trait there as with my own, i. e.—eggs in large numbers when most wanted.

In my experience I have found the Whites to lay the best, with Buffs second and Blacks next. For an all-around fowl, the Whites are probably preferable for the largest number of people in all localities.

In the old days it was very difficult to breed the Whites free from creaminess and the males became very brassy; we are now breeding them as white as the Rocks.

The Blacks are grand birds for size, type and plumage, and when bred free from purple barring (which sometimes appears), they are truly beautiful and stand without an equal.

I do not like the tendency of some of the breeders,

FIRST PRIZE CKRL & FIRST PRIZE PULLET S-C-W-ORPINGTONS BOSTON 1910.
OWEN FARMS   VINEYARD HAVEN, MASS.

especially Western fanciers who are breeding them very cobby, and I think, a bit too low. I like a low bird, but think one of their size needs some length of leg and should stand a little distance from the ground, to show off well and do best.

Then, I dislike poor color in Blacks, as much as in the Whites if not more so, and think we should strive for better colored specimens; next to type, color should play an important part, but is unfortunately too often disregarded.

They are all good sitters and make excellent mothers. As a table fowl they are unsurpassable. We have had farmers who never heard of Orpingtons before, eat at our table, and remark, about the excellent quality of the fowls. Given a Black Orpington cockerel, weighing 8 to 10 pounds, roasted, and you have all one can desire.

I always dislike to kill them, still the eating almost makes one forget the unpleasant act. When dressed they are clean and white, and once used to their appearance, the yellow, oily skin of other breeds does not appeal to one any more.

We have only to look through the poultry papers to see how the Orpingtons are coming into favor. Where only a few years ago there was but a few fanciers breeding them, now there are hundreds all over the country, and where the competition at poultry shows a few years back was between a very few, scarcely more than one or two fanciers, and then only at the largest shows, now a host of breeders are striving for the honors, and every small show has its full share of Orpington entries.

Truly they are a grand breed and too much good cannot be said about them.

English White Orpingtons

Views of a Noted Breeder and Writer on the Origin, History and Value of White Orpingtons

W. W. Broomhead, England

IT HAS always been a matter of conjecture as to how the White Orpington was "manufactured" and it is still a much debated point as to who actually brought it out. The late Mr. William Cook, who originated the Orpington fowl, claimed the honor of producing the White; and he stated that the variety was the result of Black Hamburgh hens mated with White Leghorn cocks, and their off-spring eventually crossed with White Dorkings. The first specimens bearing the name—and I refer to those produced in 1889—were, however, of a slim build and too closely resembled fowls of the non-sitting type. They did not, as a matter of fact, conform to the type of the original Orpingtons, the Blacks, which came into existence about two and a half years prior to the date mentioned. And, moreover, whereas the Blacks were single-combed, these first Whites had rose combs.

But there are other fanciers who contend that they originated the White; and, in one instance at least, in a much more simple manner—namely, from sports from the Buff. And I greatly question if there are many, if any, strains of White Orpingtons among those that are to the front at the present day in the exhibition arena which have been other than Buff bred. Some authorities, I am aware, hold different opinions; but even now it is by no means rare to find traces of the Buff ancestors in some show specimens.

Although, as I say, the White made its debut in 1889, it was rarely met with for some years after that date; and I believe that had it not been for an attempt to boom another new breed the White Orpington would have been practically unknown in the Fancy for much longer than it was. Its first revival came in 1899, during which year the Albion fowl was being boomed. This new fowl, it was stated, was a pure Sussex breed, produced solely from the existing Sussex poultry, which at that time were nothing better, as regards external points, than farm-yard fowls. However, the Albion greatly resembled the true Orpington type; hence after a season or so the Albion disappeared from the list of our breeds and the White Orpington came to the front.

For a brief period it flourished; but once again it dropped into obscurity. At the time there existed a great prejudice against white plumaged fowls of any breed. They were supposed to be delicate, and, on the other hand, it was considered a trouble to keep their plumage in a fit state for the show pen. But what the White Orpington lacked was a club to look after its interests. This, however, it obtained in 1903, when the Variety Orpington Club was formed at Crystal Palace Show, and since that time it has gone ahead in a satisfactory manner. And it became such a favorite that in 1905 breeders of the variety were numerous enough to form the White Orpington Club. That it is now a popular variety is beyond dispute, and at the recent club show at the Palace there were some two hundred entries in the eight classes. As regards its exhibition points there is not much to be said. We all know that a white bird should be white, but it is a great mistake to sacrifice other points for color. I like a good white plumage, but in my opinion type and general characteristics are much more preferable, and until true shape and the desired size are firmly fixed, it is folly to let the color faddist have full swing.

The quality of the specimens at the recent club show was certainly an improvement on last year's display; but even now there are too few really typical Whites about. The pullets, as regards shape, are better than the cockerels, which in many respects resemble Plymouth Rocks. But an adult Orpington, no matter of what variety, should not show its thighs. Then again, in the females, there is room for improvement. Some strains, too, often show blue colored shanks; but white legs are required.

As a fancier's fowl, however, the White Orpington is gaining rapidly in popularity; and since it retains its utility points, being a very good all-around fowl, it is being much sought after by those poultry keepers who do not aim at keeping exhibition specimens. It is certainly not a variety to be kept in a busy manufacturing district, since nothing looks worse than a dirty plumaged white fowl of any breed; but for a country neighborhood which is free from smoke, the White Orpington will be found to meet all the requirements for utility purposes. The eggs are large and brown shelled and the chickens can be well fed for table.—Illustrated Poultry Record.

CHAPTER VI

Non-Standard Varieties

Rose Comb Black, Buff and White; Jubilee, Spangled, Cuckoo Blue and Ermine
or Columbian Orpingtons

J. H. Drevenstedt

 NCE a new breed becomes popular, the work of producing sub-varieties begins. Scarcely had the original Black Orpington become established and recognized as a race of fowl, when the Buffs and Whites appeared. All other sub-varieties are still outside the breastworks and of the eight non-standard varieties few will eventually be admitted to the Standard, if the present temper and conservative attitude of Orpington fanciers are reliable indications.

With the exception of the Ermine or Columbian Orpington, all other sub-varieties originated in England, so the following comments by that eminent English authority, E. Campbell, in his book, "The Orpingtons," prove timely and interesting.

"For the Diamond Jubilee or Spangled Orpington I am unable to raise any great enthusiasm. A multipliance of varieties may be all right from an originator's point of view, but they need something more than these have to recommend them, to justify the breeder taking either up in face of many other beautiful and distinctive breeds.

"Nor can I say much more for the attempt to perpetuate the rose-combed varieties. Popular fancy has fixed on the single-comb as the badge of the Orpington tribe, and even though breeders would have been probably as ready to adopt the rose-comb had it arrived first, or with better specimens. The reverse being the case, it is only reasonable to suggest that rose-combs should be conceded as the Wyandotte's birthright, just as the yellow leg is the chief distinguishing mark between the Buff Rock and Buff Orpington."

Rose Combed Orpingtons

As Rose Combs appeared in the flock of Single Combed Black, Buff and White Orpingtons, not infre-

JUBILEE ORPINGTONS
Reproduced from "Feathered World," England

quently, it did not take long to establish such rose combed sports as a variety of either of these three single combed ancestors, but the demand for them was never very large, in fact, their existence today rests with a few large breed-

CUCKOO ORPINGTONS
Reproduced from "Feathered World," England

ers who by persistent advertising and exhibiting keep these Rose Combed varieties alive.

As Mr. Campbell remarked above, the "Rose Combs should be conceded as the Wyandotte's birthright." With Wyandotte breeders favoring large, blocky birds that resemble the Orpington more in type than they do the true Wyandotte, about the only difference between the ultra fashionable Black, Buff and White Wyandotte and Rose Combed Orpingtons of the same colors is in the color of the skin and shanks, and in the shape and fixture of the comb, which is larger, coarser and more corrugated in the Orpington. In size, shape and color Rose Combed Orpingtons are identical with the Single Combed varieties, the rules for breeding exhibition specimens applying to both families.

Jubilee Orpingtons

This new variety of the Orpington fowl, rarely seen in America, has enjoyed temporary popularity in England, were it originated. We are indebted to the "Illustrated Poultry Record," England, 1908, for the following comments by W. W. Broomhead, on Jubilee Orpingtons:

"The Diamond Jubilee, to give its full title, was introduced during the sixtieth year of the reign of the late Queen Victoria—hence its name. Nevertheless, its original cognomen was not a pleasing one in the Fancy, consequently the variety has for some years been known simply as the Jubilee, which name, it must be admitted, is awkward enough. There is much in a name when it is applied to a race of fowls, and I am firmly convinced that the very name Jubilee has tended in no small measure to prevent the variety becoming as popular as its good qualities merit. It is a difficult title for the public to grasp; and, moreover, it does not convey the slightest notion as to the color. Had it been christened the spangled, or even the speckled, it would undoubtedly have had a much greater vogue, since it is a really handsome fowl, and one which will provide the true fancier with ample scope for his talent.

"For some years after its introduction the Jubilee was practically unknown to the general fancier, and it was not much exhibited until the Variety Orpington Club was started in 1903. It was said to have been extensively bred prior to the latter year; but this is very questionable—if the extensive breeding refers to the variety under its new name.

"As a matter of fact, the early specimens exhibited as Diamond Jubilee Orpingtons greatly resembled a somewhat nondescript race of fowls which was common in the old days in the southeastern counties of England, and which has recently been evolved into the Speckled Sussex. To put it in plainer language, the Jubilee is merely an 'improvement'—if I may be permitted to use the word without in any way wishing to disparage the beauties of our ancient races of poultry —of the speckled farm-yard fowl indigenous to the country of Sussex. And to-day, since the Sussex Poultry Club has taken its own breed in hand for exhibition purposes, it is very difficult for the general public—aye, and the ordinary poultry fancier— to distinguish between the two varieties.

"As has been stated, its name does not give one any idea as to the color of the Jubilee; it is a parti-colored variety. The ideal aims at a combination of black, white and mahogany—bright mahogany, not a dark or maroon shade. The cock's neck and saddle hackles, back and wing bows, should be of the desired mahogany shade, with black center striping and a white tip to each feather. The wing bars should be black, the secondaries and flights of the three colors, the sickles and true tail feathers white, or black and white, or the three colors, the coverts black edged with mahogany and tipped with white. The remainder of the plumage is mahogany with black spangles and white tips, the three colors showing in equal proportions, avoiding a ticked effect on the one hand and a blotchy effect on the other. The hen is of similar colors, allowing for the usual sexual difference. The Standard notwithstanding, it is a great mistake to insist on the equality of the three colors in the hen and on the cock's breast, since it has a decided blotchy effect."

SPANGLED ORPINGTON COCK
Reproduced from "Feathered World," England

Spangled Orpingtons

Of the new variety W. H. Cook in "The Orpington and Its Varieties" writes as follows:

"This variety of the Orpington family was placed before the public early in 1900, and owing to the plumage being made up of but two colors, viz., black and white (a well-known brand), they immediately appealed to the buying public and soon made great headway, particularly in the exhibition world, as poultry people at once saw in them a very fine fowl, handsome in appearance and easy to breed true to their respective markings.

"They are somewhat larger than the Jubilee Orpingtons, being quite their equal as layers and table birds, extremely hardy and most vigorous. The pullets forage well, and a flock of them running in a field have the appearance of Anconas, but are double their size, without the objectionable yellow in the legs.

"They are perhaps not quite so cobby in build as the Jubilees, having rather a longer body, therefore carrying a good long breast and pure white flesh, which has made them popular for utility purposes. Their red comb, face and wattles, make a striking contrast to their black plumage ticked with white, and although there are many varieties of black and white fowls on the market, none are similar in markings to the Spangled Orpingtons.

"Considering the short space of time that has elapsed since their first introduction, it is surprising how many persons are to be found keeping this variety, and each year they a r e certainly becoming more widely known and popular, so much so that a separate club called the "Spangled Orpington Club" has been formed and is now on a very promising footing, with some sixty members.

"The Spangled Orpingtons were first thought of by their originator in saving sports that came pure black and white from the Jubilee Orpingtons. These were divided, part being mated to very dark colored Dark Dorking cocks, and the others to large Black Orpington cocks; the results of this mating were then re-mated together, and their progeny produced the present-day Spangles. The ground color is a beautiful beetle black, each feather being tipped or spangled with white, the tail in the cock corresponding to the body color, whereas in the hens it is almost all black, only occasionally showing a little white. The legs and feet are mottled with black and white, and the darker the coloring of the bird, the more black is produced in the legs, and though a black-legged bird is often placed in the money at shows, if all were bred with a pure white leg, as was the originator's intention, the contrast of same is more pleasing to the eye, and certainly far more useful as a table bird. It is hoped that in time the breeders of the Spangled Orpingtons will breed only for a pure white leg, or as little black in them as possible.

"The comb should be low set and well serrated, upright in the cocks; but the hens being such extraordinary layers, they invariably have a rather larger comb, ofttimes falling to one side."

In weight the cocks when developed are 10 lbs., and hens 8½ lbs., though many specimens have far exceeded these weights.

Double mating is not necessary, though some breeders resort to it, but equally good birds are produced from the one mating. Care, however, should be exercised in selecting cocks on the dark side mated to hens with an even, but not excessive, spangling all over.

As this variety are inclined to produce white in lobe, breed only from such birds as have a sound red lobe, particularly in the cocks, as any white in lobe detracts a lot of points from their appearance.

Value of Points	Deduct up to
Head	15
Color and plumage	35
Condition	15
Legs and feet	10
Size and type	25
A perfect bird to count	100

Serious Defects.

Much white in lobe, side spikes on comb, any straw, red or brown markings in the plumage.

CUCKOO ORPINGTONS

The originator, William H. Cook, gives the following history and description of Cuckoo Orpingtons in "The Orpington and Its Varieties," England, 1908:

"Quite the newest of the Orpington family is the above variety, introduced by William H. Cook early in 1907. Though classes, including the "Dairy Show," have already been provided for them, their originator's aim is not so much an exhibition specimen, as a bird possessing great utility qualities, combining a very big deep body on low legs, with absolutely first-class laying propensities. For any breed to make headway, the latter qualities are naturally most essential, and these having been attained, popularity will soon assist them to go ahead in the exhibition pen. As proof of this, seventeen birds were staged at the 1908 "Dairy Show." This as the third time that classes have been provided since their introduction to the public, is fair proof that already the variety has found favor.

"Many new members gave their patronage to the club, which has been formed to further the interests and push the Cuckoo Orpingtons.

"In appearance the 'Cuckoos' are, at first sight, similar to a barred Plymouth Rock, without the objectionable long yellow legs, which have been replaced by a perfectly pure white short pair. The skin and flesh are snow white, another great advantage in their favor, and the back is very short and broad, whilst their general shape is the blocky type that has made the Orpington family so conspicuous over other varieties of poultry. For hardiness, perhaps they are unequalled, and being splendid layers of a somewhat unusually large brown egg, they will undoubtedly recommend themselves to both fanciers and utility poultry keepers. Double mating is not at all necessary, so that anyone contemplating giving Cuckoo Orpingtons a trial can,

by purchasing just a trio of them, work up a very nice foundation stock for further developments. They will thrive and do splendidly in any nook or corner, whether on a cold clay soil or on ashes, so that amateurs need not hesitate in taking them up, and just one trio does not take up a lot of room. One will often find that "something new" in the chicken world is taken up at the start merely for curiosity and just for the sake of being in the fashion; but as soon as the "something new" is proved a poor layer, delicate or hard to breed true, they are quickly disposed of and soon forgotten.

"The originator of the Cuckoo Orpington has carefully considered these defects, and has, in introducing the 'Cuckoos,' aimed at a bird that, once tried, will be always retained."

STANDARD
General Characteristics of Cock

Head.—Small, neat and carried erect. Beak: strong and nicely curved. Eye: bold, bright and intelligent. Comb: single, fairly small, erect, evenly serrated and free from side sprigs. Ear-lobes: small. Wattles: medium length and well rounded. Neck: nicely curved, compact with full hackle.

Body.—Breast: broad, deep, and full (not flat), with long straight breast bone. Back: short and broad. Saddle: rising slightly, with full flowing hackle. Wings: nicely formed and carried close. Skin and Flesh: white, fine in texture and firm. Tail: short and compact, flowing and inclined backwards.

Legs and Feet.—Thighs and Shanks: short, strong and well set apart. Toes: four in number and well spread.

General Shape and Carriage.—Cobby and compact, erect and graceful.

Size and Weight.—Large. From 10 lbs. to 13 lbs. when fully matured.

General Characteristics of Hen

Head, Neck, Body, Legs, Feet, Skin, and Flesh—Corresponding with cock.

Tail.—Neat, small and inclined backwards with a gentle rise.

Size and Weight.—Large. From 7½ lbs. to 10 lbs.

Color

Beak: white. Eye: red. Comb and Wattles: red. Face: red, free from any trace of white. Lobes: red, no white whatever allowed. Legs: white or white mottled with black, but white preferred. Toe nails: white. Plumage: light bluish-grey ground, each feather being barred across with a darker blue-black, proportioned to the size of the feather, and the same on all parts of the body.

Value of Points
Cock or Hen

	Deduct up to
Defects in condition	10
" " color and plumage	25
" " head	10
" " want of shape	15
" " want of size	20
" " legs and feet	10
" " saddle and back	5
" " skin and flesh	5
A perfect bird to count	100

Serious Defects

Any feather or fluff on legs; long legs; any yellow on legs and feet; more than four toes; side spikes on comb; white in lobes, any deformity.

Ermine or Columbian Orpingtons

Story of the Origin of a New Variety of Orpington Produced in America by the Originator

Angier L. Goodwin

THE Ermine Orpington, the latest of the new varieties of poultry to become recognized in this country, originated in my yards in Fairfield, Maine, and Melrose, Massachusetts. One of my regular Orpington matings produced a "sport" chicken which developed into a cockerel of strikingly good Orpington type, but in color resembling a fairly-well marked Light Brahma. The exact parentage of this bird cannot be told. He may have been a "sport" from the White Orpingtons or from the Blacks, or possibly resulted from an accidental cross between the two, or between one of them and the Buffs. One thing is certain, he was an Orpington, and all Orpington.

This cockerel impressed me with the idea that if I could produce the strikingly handsome colors of the Light Brahma upon the low-built massive form of the Orpington, I would have a combination that was well worth striving for. I mated him with a pen of choice White Orpington hens, selecting with two things especially in mind, viz., trap-nest record and true Orpington type. This mating resulted in practically all pure white birds. I did get three nice-colored cockerels which were kept for next

year's matings, and several good-colored pullets were added to the original female stock. By using females of true Orpington type and from the fact that no foreign blood entered into any of the crosses on either side, it has not been necessary at any stage of the matings to cull out

severely for non-Orpington type. Each succeeding cross has made a distinct advance in color, so I now feel that it is time to give the new Orpington to the public and expedite a general introduction of the variety.

First Time Shown

I took a pen of Ermines to the Boston Show, January 12 to 16, 1909, and it is a modest estimate to say that the display was one of the features of this big exhibition.

ERMINE ORPINGTON HEN

Ideal Color Markings of the Ermine or Columbian Orpington Female, illustrated expressly for "The Orpingtons" by A. O. Schilling.

Not only prominent Orpington men, but leading breeders of many different varieties were earnest in their expression of praise and congratulation. It should be said that in color, the Ermines are not yet all that they ought to be, and for this reason, do not compare over-favorably with the old established Light Brahma; and those who believe that a new variety of poultry should not be exhibited until color points are perfected, naturally refuse to become enthusiastic over the Ermines as seen at the show. The compliments came and continue to come, from those who are disposed to be willing to see the possibilities in an Orpington, the handsomest fowl of all in type, shape and carriage, clothed in the plumage of the Light Brahma, for fifty years admitted to be the most striking color combination which nature conceived.

As to Utility

It must be apparent that the new Orpington, in beauty, can pass unchallenged. As to its utility value I believe

ERMINE ORPINGTON COCK

Ideal Color Markings of the Ermine or Columbian Orpington Male, illustrated expressly for "The Orpingtons" by A. O. Schilling.

it is sufficient to recall that the Ermine is largely, if not entirely, White Orpington as to blood lines. After a number of years' breeding Buff, Black, White and Jubilee Orpingtons side by side, I found that the Whites were in the lead as egg producers. I believe this is the experience of all who have tried all varieties of the breed. Certainly it is true as to my own strain of Whites, and it is from this champion strain that the Ermines have been "made."

Why Not "Columbian" Orpingtons

I have been asked over and over again why I do not call the new Orpington "Columbian." The best answer I can make is that this may even yet be done. When the idea of a Light Brahma-colored Orpington first entered my head, the Columbian Wyandotte boom was still in its infancy and Columbian Rocks were practically unheard of. The Wyandotte of this color was called "Columbian" for the reason that it was brought out during the year of the Columbian Exposition. It can hardly be denied that naming a variety of poultry after an advent in history is more or less absurd. But now that the variety has attained wide popularity and the Columbian Rock is steadily gaining ground, with rumors of a Columbian Leghorn well under way, it is entirely possible that as a matter of policy, the name "Columbian" is the best one to be used for any new variety of poultry bearing the colors of the Light Brahma.

I chose the name Ermine for the reason that it means something. Webster says: "Ermine (pronounced er-min) a fur bearing animal—white except the tip of the tail, which is always black." Also "the fur of the ermine as prepared for ornamenting garments of royalty, etc., by having the tips of the tail, which are black, arranged at regular intervals throughout the white." Fowldom has already had the Ermine Faverolle, the Ermine Antwerp-Brahma, the Ermine Huttegem (the two latter Belgian breeds) and the Erminette.

So marked do I find the feeling among many of those who have become interested in the new Orpington that it should be called "Columbian," that I deem it advisable to say here that one of the first duties of the Club which is now in process of formation to promote and popularize the new variety will be to decide upon which is the better name, under all of the circumstances, to be used.

BLUE ORPINGTONS

This new variety was produced in England several years ago, but few specimens have been exhibited up to the present time. In shape and size it resembles its White and Black Orpington ancestors; in color the same markings as found in Blue Andalusians and Blue Wyandottes will be adopted as Standard color. The latter in the Blue Orpington male is—Head, Hackle, Back and Saddle: Rich lustrous black, without lacing. Breast and Thighs: Clear silver blue in ground color, with distinct black lacing on each feather. Shoulders and wing-bows: Rich lustrous black. Wing-bars: Same as body, with well-defined lacing on outer edges. Secondaries and Flight Feathers and Main Tail Feathers: Same color as the breast, the secondaries laced if possible. Sickle Feathers and Tail Coverts: Purplish black. In the hen—Head and Hackle: Rich lustrous black without lacing in upper hackle, but showing broad lacing on tips of the feathers at the base. Breast, Body, Back and Thighs: Same silver blue ground color as the male's breast with distinct black lacing on each feather. The wing-bars should have well defined lacing; the secondaries edged or laced if possible. Tail: Same as the body with the ends laced up if possible. Beak and Shanks and Feet: Dark slate.

WINNER OF FIRST PRIZE, NEW YORK, DEC 28 1909 JAN 1 1910
BRED AND OWNED BY   MOUNTAIN VIEW FARM
E.A. HARING, PROPR   SOUTH KENT, CONN, U.S.A.

BLACK ORPINGTON PULLET

CHAPTER VII

Orpingtons As Exhibition Fowl

Judging Orpingtons by the Score Card—Instructions in Scoring as Practiced by Judges in the Show Room

D. E. Hale

IN scoring Orpingtons the same system is used as in other breeds, and which has been explained many times in the poultry press, but for the benefit of those who have never had the benefit of that instruction we will say that a perfect bird is represented as being worth one hundred points. The fowl, as represented on the score-card is divided into fifteen different sections, each section valued at a certain amount, as listed in the scale of points given below. In scoring, the specimen is examined, first as a whole, which is called symmetry, and then each individual section is examined for shape and color defects and whatever per cent. the judge thinks the specimen is lacking from being perfect, is deducted from the valuation of that section and the amount of the deduction, generally called a "cut," is written on the score-card. The total of these cuts deducted from one hundred gives us the score of the fowl.

The official score-card of the American Poultry Association revised at the annual meeting of the latter, held at Niagara Falls, August, 1909, is divided into the following sections:

OFFICIAL SCORE CARD OF THE AMERICAN POULTRY ASSOCIATION

Exhibitor ....
Breed .... Sex ....
Entry No. .... Band No. .... Weight.............

	SHAPE	COLOR	REMARKS
Symmetry			
Weight			
Size			
Condition			
Comb			
Head			
Beak			
Eyes			
Lobes			
Wattles			
Neck			
Back			
Tail			
Wings			
Breast			
Body and Fluff			
Legs			
Toes			
Crest and Beard			
Shortness of Feather			
Cuts			Score

Judge ....
Secretary ....

The last two sections, "Crest and Beard" and "Shortness of Feather," apply to crested breeds and games and game bantams only.

In order to give some idea as to what we are doing in applying these valuations, etc., we must quote from the Standard the scale of points as applied to Orpingtons.

Scale of Points

Symmetry	4
Weight	6
Condition	4
Comb	8
Head—Shape, 2, Color 2....................	4
Beak—Shape 2, Color 2......................	4
Eyes—Shape 2, Color 2......................	4
Wattles and Ear-lobes—Shape 2, Color 3......	5
Neck—Shape 4, Color 4......................	8
Back—Shape 5, Color 5......................	10
Breast—Shape 5, Color 5....................	10
Body and Fluff—Shape 5, Color 3............	8
Wings—Shape 4, Color 4....................	8
Tail—Shape 5, Color 4......................	9
Legs and Toes—Shape 5, Color 3............	8
Total	100

Symmetry

The first section in the scale of points is symmetry. Webster defines symmetry as "A due proportion of the several parts of a body to each other; or the union and conformity of the members of a work to the whole." In comparison judging and upon some score-cards it is shown as "typical carriage," which is defined in the Standard as "expressing a characteristic, in color or form, representative of the breed or variety." "Representative of the breed or variety,"—please remember that, as it is the main point we wish to make.

This section always has been the subject of discussion, but if we understand the Standard requirements of a fowl and study each section, also their general outline, how the parts or sections should fit together in harmony—in fact, get the ideal shape fixed in our mind as shown in the Standard drawings and descriptions—then the minute we get a good look at a bird we know whether it is typical of the breed it represents or has symmetry.

In Orpingtons we have a breed that is described as "large and stately in appearance." Their bodies are rather long, round and deep while the breast should be full, round and deep. The backs are broad and moderately long; the abundance of the hackle and saddle feathers giving it a rather short appearance. The body should be broad and deep with a rather long, straight keel-bone extending well forward, the fluff being moderately full. The wing-fronts should be well covered with the breast feathers and the tips by the saddle feathers. The tail is only moderately long, well spread and carried at an angle of 45 degrees from the horizontal and should be coupled with the back so that there is no apparent angle where these sections join. The sickles are of medium length, extending beyond the tail feathers, while the lesser sickles and tail coverts are also described as moderately long. The thighs are rather short and large, covered with soft feathers; the shanks short, smooth and stout in bone and should be free from feathers or down. The toes are of medium length, straight, strong and well spread.

Now let us take the time and space to look at a specimen and see what defects we want to look for when judging the symmetry of a fowl. Remember we have here a broad and deep fowl with a moderate length; the intentions of the breeders are to maintain the cobby appearance. Is its head too long and narrow, or as some express it, "snaky?" Is it caused by the beak being long and straight instead of curved, or is it really the head? Is the neck too long and scantily feathered, or as we hear it expressed in the show room parlance, "not filled?" You need not worry about the neck of an Orpington being too short.

If a male: Is the neck well arched and the hackle well feathered so that it connects or flows onto the shoulders or back in a graceful curve? Are the shoulders broad and flat, or are they narrow and high? Has he a nice broad saddle, well feathered, connecting with a tail that is well spread at the base; or is it narrow and flat, giving the tail a narrow, pinched appearance? Is his breast full, broad, round and deep, or is it narrow and flat? Are his legs good, firm, stocky legs, well spread so that you can get the width of your hand between them, or are they long, slim and knock-kneed? You will soon get so that you will notice these good and bad points at a glance and make up your mind in an instant whether the specimen should be cut one-half or one and one-half. A successful judge must think and act quickly. The minute you begin to hesitate as to a cut you begin to fail.

Remember this section is worth four points and when you cut a bird one for symmetry you mean it is one-fourth or twenty-five per cent. to the bad. There is no system that we know of that can be successfully applied. The best way is to use your own judgment. You know this section is worth four points and when you are judging symmetry, just forget that there is any other section to the bird; no matter if some exhibitor does tell you that you are cutting twice. Judge the bird as a whole and deduct whatever you think is lacking from perfection. If four points represent one hundred in this section, all right. If the bird is in your judgment 25 per cent. off, cut it one point for symmetry. They tell us: "It is like a two-edged sword, cutting both ways." One for symmetry because the bird has a bad tail or a bad breast, and then cutting these sections again for shape when we come to them. That is not true. If symmetry is worth four points and breast five points for shape, we are not cutting twice. If you do not use this section of symmetry in scoring your specimen, then you should deduct your total cuts from ninety-six instead of one hundred.

Weight

The Standard weights were given the different breeds because it was found that they were at their best as a commercial product when at the weights specified in the Standard. The weights on the Orpingtons were not changed at the recent revision of the Standard. Neither were the instructions which said that for every pound under the Standard weight cut two points; one-fourth pound to be the minimum. For example, if a fowl is one pound underweight it should be cut one point, and if one-fourth pound light it should be cut one-half point. One

new ruling worthy of remembrance is that a fowl two or more pounds under Standard weight will not be considered, or in other words will be disqualified.

Disqualifications and Shape

Up to this point you have not found it necessary to take the specimen out of the cage. It might be well to take notice of a few things before doing so and perhaps save the extra work of handling the bird. Side sprigs on the comb disqualify and may sometimes be noticed when you glance at the bird in getting its symmetry cuts. "Squirrel tails" and "decidedly wry tails" also disqualify and will be noticed before handling a specimen. In judging the symmetry and shape of a bird we believe that it should be done in as quiet a manner as possible so as not to disturb the fowl and get it in as natural a position as possible. Walk up to the cage as quietly as possible and without disturbing the bird at all, if it can be helped, get your impression of the fowl's symmetry and shape cuts in

BUFF ORPINGTON WINNERS, 1900-01

breast, back, tail, neck, legs and toes. If the bird is standing or crowded into a corner or against the sides of the cage so that it is out of shape, reach in with your stick, not to poke him, but gently crowd him out into the center of the cage, smooth his neck and back with your judging stick and it will, ninety-nine times out of one hundred, with such treatment, act or pose in a natural manner. Then its symmetry cuts can be gotten quickly.

Cutting for Shape

In getting the shape of a fowl and cutting the different defects we proceed as follows: If we think the neck is too long and "not filled," or in other words, full of immature feathers, giving it a scrawny appearance, the cut is from one-half to one. If the back, which is worth five points for shape, is too long, too narrow, too flat, saddle not filled, too narrow at shoulders, etc., we cut from one-half to three. If a crooked back is detected the specimen is disqualified. Now look at the tail and see if it is carried at a right angle. Is it well-spread and well filled? For example, a female's tail should have seven feathers on each side. If you will examine the Standard drawings you will note that a little of each feather shows when viewed from the side. This is called a well-spread tail from a side view, and when viewed from the rear it will resemble an inverted V. When viewed from the top or front it should look broad and full, sloping from the saddle with a concave sweep. Should there be an angle at the base of and in front of the tail, it is probably caused by the tail being carried too high and should be cut from one-half to one and one-half.

Now the breast, which is an important section in determining the true Orpington shape. If it is flat and narrow, and looks immature and not filled out, it should be cut from one-half to three.

Remember the body should be broad and deep with a keel-bone that is rather long and straight and carried well forward, with a fluff that is moderately full. If too short and shallow, giving a Wyandotte or Plymouth Rock appearance, it should be cut from one-half to one and one-half.

Look at the legs and toes before taking the bird out, as well as after. See if it is knock-kneed, bow-legged, too long in legs or has crooked toes. Legs too long are cut from one-half to one and one-half. Crooked toes are cut one-half point each. Missing spurs on cock birds cut one-half point each.

In looking at the wings, it is well to hold your cuts for shape until you have the fowl out of the cage. You should, however, see that the wings are carried in a proper position and not slipped. By slipped wings we mean ones where the primaries fall or hang down and are not "tucked up" under the secondaries as they should be. This is caused sometimes by a feather or two being missing where the primaries and secondaries are connected; or it is sometimes caused by muscular weakness. It should be cut from one to three points, depending on whether it is one or both wings that are slipped. This is a serious defect as it will reproduce itself and really should, in our opinion, be made a disqualification. It should, therefore, be cut hard enough to throw the specimen out of competition to discourage the breeding of such specimens.

Now we are ready to take the specimen out of the cage and examine it for color and other defects. Do not reach in and grab the fowl by legs and drag it out feet first, thus taking chances on breaking wing feathers. Take hold of one wing, from in front, near the front or body, and you can turn the bird in any position you wish. Then lead it out of the cage and as you do so, with your other hand grasp its legs at the hock joint, letting the bird's body rest on your arm. The fowl is thus held securely and comfortably and can be easily handled without injury.

Condition

The next section we notice on the score-card is condition. It is valued at four points and is one of the most difficult sections on the list to explain in writing. No definite rule can be laid down for cutting defects found under this section. The judge has here got to show his wisdom and "horse sense." He has to be familiar with the different diseases, the effects of freezing or frost-bite, the effects of cuts, injuries, etc., and dirty and broken plumage, or whether there is poor condition from over feeding or starving. Condition, as referred to in the Standard, means: "The state of a fowl as regards health, cleanliness and order of plumage." Some birds will catch a slight cold when being shipped to a show and just begin to show it when judged. In these cases the judge will generally

consider the specimen, cutting it from one-half to one and one-half. If, however, the bird has a well-defined case of roup or other contagious disease, it should at once be removed from the show room. If the superintendent has not noticed it before the judge gets to it, it is the judge's duty to notify him at once and insist upon the fowl being removed from the room. Frosted combs and wattles should receive a cut of from one-half to two, depending upon whether they are just slightly frosted or whether they are festered.

Soiled plumage that looks as if the exhibitor had made no effort to get the bird in good show condition, should be cut one to two points. If it looks as if it had been cleaned up in nice shape and had become soiled in shipping to the show, the judge can be a little lenient with such a specimen.

If the bird is too fat from over feeding to get it up in weight, dropping the body and fluff below the hock line, it should be cut from one to two points.

Scaly Legs

There is no excuse whatever for showing a bird with scaly legs, because it is so easily cured. A good scrubbing with hot water and soap, then a little kerosene, lard or vaseline applied twice a week for two weeks will cure the worst case that ever existed.

Head—Beak—Eyes—Wattles and Ear-lobes

Head is the next section and valued at four points each, divided two each for shape and color.

The head is rather large, broad and deep, while the beak is short and stout and nicely curved; the eyes being large and oval in shape. If the head is long, slim or narrow it should be cut one-half to one. A straight beak, giving it a long, slender appearance should be cut one-half to one as in degree. Deformed beaks will disqualify. If blind in one eye, cut one. If the eye has run out leaving only the socket, cut one and one-half.

The wattles and ear-lobes are valued at five points, two for shape and three for color. The wattles should be fine in texture, of medium length and well rounded at the bottoms. Should they be coarse, cut one-half. Should they be torn from fighting or other injury the cut should be one-half to one and one-half as in degree. Should they be folded or wrinkled, cut from one-half to one. The ear-lobes should be oblong in shape and fine in texture. Coarse or wrinkled lobes should be cut from one-half to one. Color cuts for these sections are described under each variety color explanation.

Comb

The comb is valued at eight points. It is an important section, as is shown by its high valuation with only shape to be considered. The Orpington comb is somewhat larger or coarser than the ordinary single comb. It really should be fine in texture, but the larger size gives it a rather coarse appearance. It should have five well-defined points or serrations with the front and rear ones lower than those in the center. The base should be solid and set firmly upon the head in order to give the comb an upright carriage. Side sprigs disqualify as does also a lopped comb. A lopped single comb must fall over so that the points are below the horizontal plane where the comb begins to lop. Too many breeders seem to think that all there is to a comb is the serrations. You will hear many of them make the remark that "there is a good comb: it has five points" or "there is a bad comb; it has only four or six points," as the case may be. The Standard says that for every serration more or less than five we shall cut one-half point. Supposing the fowl had lost all of its points or serrations it would only be cut two and one-half and we would still have a valuation of five and one-half to apply to the rest of the comb. Let us look at some of the other defects. Thumb marks, which are a sort of indentation or hollow place in the side of the comb, should be cut not less than one point. Comb turning at the rear should be cut from one-half to one and one-half, as in degree. Irregularity of serrations, cut from one-half to one. Irregularity or rough-edged blade, cut from one-half to one. "Beefy" or large and overgrown at junction of beak, generally causing wrinkles, cut one-half to one. You see there are quite a lot of defects to look for in a comb and it is a section that is worthy of considerable study.

Neck

The neck section is valued at eight points, divided four for shape and four for color. The neck should be rather short and well arched and tapering nicely to the head, with hackle enough to give it a full appearance. The cuts for shape are explained under "Disqualifications and Shape" and the color defects will be handled under each variety for color.

Back

This section has a valuation of ten points, five each for shape and color. Remember that the back should be broad and moderately long, rising with a concave sweep to the tail. The breadth of the back and the abundant hackle and saddle feathers are rather deceiving to the eye as regards the length. The Orpington back is really quite long, but owing to the depth and breadth and rather loose plumage it appears to be short. An Orpington without a good broad back, when viewed from the top, is not a good Orpington. Crooked backs, as mentioned before, disqualify.

If too narrow, cut from one-half to two and one-half. If too short, giving it a Wyandotte appearance, cut one-half to two and one-half. If too long and flat cut from one-half to two and one-half. If saddle plumage is broken or not well filled, causing a break at junction with tail, cut from one-half to one and one-half. If too much cushion, which would cause a Wyandotte or Cochin effect, cut one-half to two. If too narrow or high at shoulders, cut one-half to two. If too curved, giving the back a Langshan or U appearance, cut from one-half to two. Color defects and cuts will be explained under the different variety explanations.

"LADY OF THE SNOWS"
The Famous White Orpington Hen, Winner of First Prize and Bronze Medal for Best Hen in the Show, at Allentown, Pa., 1910; First Prize, Bronze Medal for Best Hen in the Show, and Silver Cup for Best Bird on Exhibition at Hagerstown, Md., 1910. Bred and Owned by Sunswick Poultry Farm.

Tail

The tail section is valued at nine points divided five for shape and four for color. It should be moderately long, well spread and carried at an angle of forty-five degrees from the horizontal. A well-spread tail is explained under "Disqualifications and Shape." Missing sickle feathers on the male (black or white) should be cut one and one-half points each. If tail is carried too high cut from one-half to two and one-half. If it is carried so high that it comes in front of an imaginary perpendicular line rising from the base of the tail, it becomes a squirrel tail and disqualifies. Pinched or "gamey" tails, or those that show only one or two feathers from a side view (especially on females) should be cut from one-half to one point. All color defects and cuts are explained under the descriptions of the different varieties.

Breast

Breast section is valued at ten points, five each for shape and color. This is one of the prominent sections of an Orpington and without a good full, deep and round breast we lack the Orpington type. The shape cuts are described under "Disqualifications and Shape" with the exception of a crooked breast or keel-bone and that we usually consider under body section. Remember that a full crop does not necessarily mean a full breast.

Body and Fluff

This is the next section and is valued at eight points, divided five for shape and three for color. Shape cuts have been described. If a crooked breast-bone or keel-bone is discovered it should be cut from one-half to two and one-half, as in degree.

Wings

This section is valued at eight points, four each for shape and color. Shape defects, with the exception of broken or missing plumage, have been described above. Broken or missing flight feathers in the Blacks or Whites should be cut one and one-half points each. In the Buffs they should be cut one-half point each.

Legs and Toes

Remember that feathers or down on shanks or toes will disqualify. Scaly legs were described above. Knock-knees or bow-legs should be cut from one-half to one and one-half as in degree.

Color Defects and Cuts

THE BLACKS. The Black variety should have a black beak; eyes should be black or dark brown, while the comb, face, wattles and ear-lobes are red. The plumage throughout should be a rich, lustrous, greenish black with a black under-color. The legs and toes are black with the web and bottoms of toes white. The skin should be white on all Orpingtons. Yellow skin on the Blacks should disqualify. Positive white covering more than one-third the surface of the ear-lobes will also disqualify. Positive white does not mean paleness in lobes, as is often seen, but what is known as enamel white—a white through which the blood cannot be made to circulate. Generally when we strike such cases we hold the bird downward for a few minutes and rub the lobe. If it is not an enamel or positive white you can generally get the blood to flush the lobes. Positive white in lobes, where not enough to disqualify, should be cut from one-half to one and one-half in each lobe. In examining plumage we must remember that one-half inch or more of white will disqualify. Purple barring should be cut from one-half to two in each section where found. Red or other foreign color should be cut from one to the color limit in each section where found. If the eyes are too light in color cut from one-half to one and one-half. A faded or dead black, especially on a male, should be cut from one-half to one in each section.

THE BUFFS. The beak, shanks and toes should be white or pinkish white. Any other color will disqualify. Positive white, as explained under the Black variety in regard to ear-lobes, will also disqualify. The plumage throughout should be an even shade of rich golden buff, free from shafting or mealy appearance. The main point is to get one harmonious shade of buff from head to tail. A lemon and cinnamon buff are given as the two extremes of light and dark, and a medium shade between these two

is desired. Different shades of buff in two or more sections is a serious defect. Mealiness in plumage should be cut from one-half to one and one-half in each section where found, as in degree. Shafting, or light colored shafts, should be cut the same—one-half to one and one-half in each section, as in degree. Different shades of buff should be cut from one-half to two and one-half. Black or white should be cut from one-half to the color limit in each section where found. Eyes too light or too dark should be cut from one-half to one and one-half. Missing or broken main tail or primaries or secondaries should be cut one-half point each. Missing sickle feathers in male should be cut one point each. Most breeders prefer black to white in wing and tail of breeding specimens, but the Standard says: "both are equally objectionable."

THE WHITES. More than one-third of the surface of ear-lobes covered with positive white will disqualify, as will also any other color than white in plumage. Legs and toes should be white or pinkish white and any other color will disqualify as will also feathers or down on shanks or toes. The most common defects found are creaminess and brassiness, the latter being more noticeable in the males as a rule. Creaminess is caused by the oil in the feathers and is used up as the feather matures. Wherever creaminess is found, cut from one-half to one and one-half in each section. Brassiness will be found on the surface only and should be cut from one to two points in each section where found. Gray specks, generally spoken of as "ticking" will be cut from one-half to two points wherever found. The white plumage should be a pure, pearl white and with the white skin there ought to be no very great trouble in breeding it.

Conditioning Orpingtons for the Show Room

Simple and Safe Methods of Preparing and Washing Exhibition Specimens

E. A. Haring

THE Orpington is an ideal show bird. It has a quiet disposition and shows off to advantage. The first thing to learn in showing birds is to know your breed, study the type until you can tell a good one at a glance. Too many breeders breed good birds occasionally and never know it until someone buys the bird for a song. Know your birds, know how many good ones you have, know for a certainty that they are free from disqualifications, then make your entries. Do not enter every bird you have that you think might win; reserve a few for emergencies; better show a few good ones than a string of ordinary ones, and above all, show only as many as you can properly fit.

Personally, I think condition should count for more in the show room than it does; first to encourage the breeders to better efforts, and second for the good of the show. It does not seem as though a true fancier would send a bird to a show of any kind., without first putting it into the best condition possible. Stock taken from the yards and shown in all their filth, collected in a season's scratching and dusting, is a poor advertisement for any breeder.

The first step is to set up some coops in a well lighted building, about three weeks before the time the show is to open; then pick your birds and place them in these coops and see how they show up. In this way you can

select the ones wanted; next make your entries—always less than the number selected. Now begin to coop, train and handle the birds and get them so tame that nothing out of the ordinary is likely to frighten them. Feed and water them regularly and keep them in good condition. About a week before the show, take a pan of warm water, soap, a small stiff brush and some good sized tooth picks, and, with someone holding the bird, and with a pan of water between you, start washing his feet and scrub them thoroughly. If very dirty remove the dirt from under the scales very carefully with the tooth picks. If old scales are loose and ready to come off, remove same. After drying rub with a very little vaseline. The birds are then ready to be washed. We make it a rule to wash all birds, Buff, Black or White and think one is improved by the process as much as the other. There is and has been much written on the subject of washing fowls. It is a very simple matter, the main points being plenty of warm water, soap and patience. A light sunny room is heated to about 90 degrees, three tubs of clean, soft water provided, and a supply of turkish towels. The first tub should contain warm water. In this the bird is held and after being made thoroughly wet, is given a good soaping with Ivory Soap, having him lathered all over, and wash it clean. It is best for one person to hold the fowl and another to do the washing; the work should not be rushed.

time being taken to do it thoroughly and, above all, do not attempt to wash too many birds in the same water. A frequent change of the wash water will repay you for your trouble. When the bird has been well washed all over and looks clean, it is put into the next tub containing water somewhat cooler and is well rinsed. Care should be taken to get all the soap out of the feathers; this is important and for this reason the bird should be put through the third tub, which in case of white birds being washed, can contain a small quantity of best quality blueing.

Then they are taken from the water and dried with a towel as well as can be, their feathers shaken out a little, and placed in the coops nearest the heat to dry. As they commence to dry they may be put into the coops a little farther away from the heat and as more are washed, they can be started drying in the warmer coops, from which the first have been taken.

It is best to have all the washing done two or three days before they are to be shipped,—gradually cool down the room as soon as they are thoroughly dry, so that when shipped to the winter shows, the birds are not taken right from the very warm room into the cold air. If the coops are kept clean, the birds will not become soiled if they must remain in there a few days after washing.

Before shipping, rub combs and wattles with a piece of sponge or cotton, moistened with sweet oil and alcohol well mixed together.

If possible be at the show to place your birds in the coops when they arrive there, but do not be found in the aisles pulling feathers, etc., as too many of our fanciers are. Have them fit before shipping, and barring accidents, they will be fit when they arrive at the show.

Do not talk with the judge or lean over his shoulder while he is judging, even if he will allow it; it does not look well, and finally, if the judge does not see your best bird in the right light and perhaps places a bird over him that should have been disqualified, swallow hard and try again. It is all in the game. Let us show the stock which is the result of our knowledge and labor in such condition that win or lose we shall be proud of it.

Orpingtons In England

Popularity of the New Breed Due to Superior Utilitarian Qualities—English Poultry Club Standards for All Varieties

Charles D. Leslie, England

WE are proud of the Orpington. A comparative upstart in the poultry world, it has, by sheer merit, won its way not only to the front rank, but to the position of the premier popular breed of Great Britain. The Phoenicians brought us the Game fowl and initiated the early Britains into the sport of cock fighting. Then came the Romans, who brought the Dorking and taught us to eat poultry; for strange though it seems, there is ample proof that poultry in pre-Roman times was kept for diversion alone and not as an article of diet. Brahmas, Cochins and Langshans came, of course, from the far East; the Spanish and Minorcas from south Europe; Leghorns, not from Italy, but the United States, which has also given us those two wonderfully popular breeds, the Rocks and the Wyandottes; but the Orpington is our very own.

By a curious coincidence, the sudden and lamented death of Mr. W. Cook—the originator of all five varieties of the Orpington fowl—which occurred nearly a year ago, synchronized with the sudden rise to popularity of White Orpingtons, which for many years had, as it were, hung fire. There are now three popular varieties in this country, the Blacks, Buffs and Whites, and two newer and less known, the Jubilee and Spangled, which are, however, steadily gaining adherents.

There have been many efforts made to produce new and original English breeds, but uniform failure has been the result, except in the experience of Mr. Cook. There is, I think, an aphorism to the effect that if you have a good thing and wish to make it known, you must understand how to advertise it. This is quite true with regard to a new breed of poultry. Mr. Cook thoroughly believed in his Orpingtons and pushed the breed vigorously until the poultry world took it up. The original Black Orpingtons says one well-known writer—were practically Langshans, meaning simply, that they had in them a great deal of Langshan blood.

Black Orpingtons are Handsome Fowls "Planned for Utility"

Having been planned for utility purposes alone, there are no fancy points about the Black Orpingtons. Handsome, they are, with their deep, broad breasts and massive bodies, but decorative, they are not. They are white skinned and make first-class table fowl, fattening early and presenting a nice appearance when dressed. The hens are good layers of brown, tinted eggs of average size, are quiet in disposition, and, although not inveterate sitters, they make good sitters and mothers when entrusted with eggs. Black Orpingtons have single combs. A rose combed variety was produced, but failed to "catch on" in popular favor. In size the Blacks are large, the cock weighing nine to eleven pounds and the hen seven to eight pounds when fully matured. Our Poultry Club's Standard for Black Orpingtons reads as follows:

Poultry Club's (England) Standard for Black Orpingtons

Defects in plumage and condition, deduct up to..10 points
Defects in head, deduct up to ....25 points
Defects in breast, saddle, back and tail, ded. up to.20 points
Defects in legs and feet, deduct up to........... 5 points
Defects in skin and flesh, deduct up to........... 5 points
Defects in carriage, deduct up to ....10 points
Want of shape, deduct up to....................15 points
Want of size, deduct up to....................10 points
———
A perfect bird to count...................100 points

Color of Black Orpingtons: Beak, black; eye, black, with dark brown iris; comb, face, ear-lobes and wattles, red; shanks, black; skin and flesh, white; plumage, black throughout, with a green sheen or luster upon it, free from colored feathers.

General characteristics: Shape and carriage should be cobby and compact, erect and graceful. The plumage should be close; tail medium; body, broad, deep, and full; thighs, short; shanks, short and strong; the single comb should be of medium size, evenly serrated and free from side sprigs; flesh, firm."

Buff Orpingtons Satisfy the British Market Demand

The people of Great Britain are much in favor of birds with white legs, in fact, a first-class table fowl must show a white shank, or else it ceases to be a first-class table fowl. As our only white-legged fowls, previous to the advent of the Buff Orpingtons, were the Dorkings and some of the Game varieties, there naturally followed a boom in that variety which has only just begun to subside. Fanciers, farmers, and suburban poultry keepers all took

WHITE ORPINGTON COCK
Winner of first prize and special at Madison Square Garden and Boston; also first at Cleveland, Ohio, 1909. Bred and owned by Sunswick Poultry Farm, South Plainfield, N. J.

them up. Since the early days of the Buff Orpington it has been wonderfully improved, but even now it is far from perfect, though feathered legs and long backs no longer appear in the show pen. It is still quite difficult to breed them anywhere true to color, and indeed, sound buff tails are yet scarce, but the utility value of the variety makes amends, as the off-colored pullets may be kept for layers and the cockerels fatted for the table.

The three points to be considered in breeding Buff Orpingtons are, first, color, which should be a sound buff, free from black and white feathers; second, shape, which should be similar to that of the Black Orpington; third, clean, white feet and shanks, free from feathering. The Poultry Club Standard differs somewhat from that for the Blacks:

Poultry Club's (England) Standard for Buff Orpingtons

Defects in head and comb, deduct up to.........10 points
Defects in color, deduct up to...................35 points
Defects in legs and feet, deduct up to...........15 points
Want of shape, deduct up to....................20 points
Want of size, deduct up to.....................10 points
Want of condition, deduct up to.................10 points
———
100

Serious defects for which Buff Orpingtons should be passed are: Other than four toes; wry tail; feathers or fluff on legs and feet; yellow skin; yellow in legs or feet; in both Blacks and Buffs, any colored feathers other than black and buff.

White Orpingtons have been in existence for nearly twenty years, but if my memory serves me, the originals were not unlike the White Minorcas. They now approach in appearance the White Dorking. I give below, the White Orpington Club Standard, which is, I believe, accepted by the Poultry Club:

The White Orpington Club (England) Standard

For cock: Comb, single, of medium size, well set upon the head, erect and free from side sprigs; eye, red; beak, short, white, and nicely curved; ear-lobes, red, small and round; wattles, well rounded, of fine texture; color, a pure, snow white, free from any foreign color; neck and saddle hackle, full and long; tail, medium size and inclined backwards; back, short and nicely curved; legs and feet, white, free from feathers, four toes on each foot, straight and set well apart; breast, broad and full.

For hen: Same color, head and type as in male bird, of neat appearance and active habits. The type in both sexes must be cobby, of low build and short on legs.

White Orpingtons are steadily increasing in favor, in some measure due to the boom in white breeds which was a feature of last year, but it is their great value as a table fowl that is chiefly responsible for the larger numbers kept. They are gradually taking the place of the White Dorking, as they are equally good as table fowl, better layers, and far hardier. Their only drawback is their color. No small proportion of British poultry keepers are town dwellers, either professional men or members of the working classes, who have only a few square yards of space to spare for the fowls. No white breed shows to advantage on bare earth runs and hence the suburban poultry keepers as a class, avoid white breeds. Even the White Leghorn, in the height of its prosperity, was not nearly so largely kept as the Black Minorca—always the chief favorite among suburban poultrymen.

In size, all Orpingtons should be as large as possible, consistent with type.

Orpingtons Are Increasing in Popularity

To this brief description of the various breeds of Orpingtons today, and its present position in the poultry world, I have little to add, but its fame is extending far beyond these Islands. Our colonies have taken it up largely, for instance, New Zealand has specially taken to the Spangles, and imports them to this country. In South Africa the Orpingtons are the most popular breed. They are not in great favor on the continent, except in Hungary, where they are bred in large numbers.

Their universal favoritism indicates very plainly the trend of popular taste toward utility as well as fancy. The days of the purely "fancy" fowls are past, such breeds as the Polish, Spanish, etc., whose attractiveness is entirely due to their quaint appearance, being practically extinct, although they were formerly the mainstay of our shows.

Orpingtons were originally bred for utility only, and although our fanciers have taken them up so warmly that at all our big poultry exhibitions they form a show of themselves, the economic qualities of the breed have not suffered, nor is there at present any chance, so far as I can see, of any other breed even seriously challenging their position in the near future.

Popularity of Orpingtons as an Exhibition Fowl

Tables Showing the Number of Each Variety Exhibited at Madison Square—Boston and Chicago from 1901 up to 1910—Tables Unobtainable Elsewhere and of Historic Interest to Orpington Breeders

D. E. Hale

MANY of the readers of these lines will remember the introduction of the Orpingtons into the United States. It was quite generally remarked at the time that the Black Orpingtons might compete on favorable terms with our other black breeds, but it was claimed that the white skin and white or pink legs would make it impossible for them to become popular as a table fowl in this country. Consequently it was predicted that their boom would be short lived.

The many prophets who made such assertions now acknowledge they were wrong and that there is something about the Orpingtons which has enabled them to steadily win their way well along toward the head of the list of breeds that bear the stamp of approval among real fanciers.

Even the old school market men are beginning to tell us that "one of the prettiest carcasses that goes on the table is that of this new English breed, the Orpington." The American public is coming to realize that a white skin may cover meat that is just as tender, just as juicy and just as fine in flavor as that covered by a yellow skin.

Probably the reader will ask: What has all this to do with the popularity of the Orpingtons as exhibition fowl? Only this: When we come to the real test of general popularity, every breed or variety must stand or fall upon its valuation as a market or table fowl. Once a breed or variety wins public favor as a commercial fowl, it will soon come to the front as an exhibition fowl. Its popularity will cause more breeders to take it up and then competition will become stronger, which leads to the show room and results in larger and still larger exhibitions.

Following is a tabulated report, showing the number of Orpingtons that have been exhibited in recent years at the Crystal Palace Show, London, at Madison Square Garden, New York, and at Boston, and Chicago. Note the growth each year in the number exhibited at these great shows.

Crystal Palace Show

	1906	1907	1908
Number shown	580	697	782

We are sorry we cannot give the number of each variety at the above show. The numbers given represent totals of all Orpingtons shown each year for the period covered.

Madison Square Garden

Year	S.C. Buff	R.C. Buff	S.C. Black	R.C. Black	S.C. White	R.C. White	Any other variety	Total
1901	27	..	4	..	..	..	..	31
1902	43	..	..	..	..	..	20	63
1903	64	4	27	21	10	..	17	143
1904 Unable to get report.								
1905	173	16	100	11	57	5	30	392
1906	192	25	105	11	73	10	30	446
1907 (Jan.)	161	18	133	10	81	5	26	434
1907 (Dec.)	107	10	160	11	83	5	26	402
1909	223	14	144	15	70	5	25	496
1910	175	12	134	8	155	20	22	526
	1165	99	807	87	529	50	196	2933

At Boston

Year	S.C. Buff	R.C. Buff	S.C. Black	R.C. Black	S.C. White	R.C. White	Any other variety	Total
1902	17	..	..	..	..	..	4	21
1903	32	..	11	..	8	..	11	62
1904 No show held.								
1905	31	..	..	..	10	..	6	47
1906	46	..	36	..	26	..	16	124
1907	67	..	15	4	21	4	10	121
1908	69	1	47	..	21	..	6	144
1909	65	..	31	..	28	..	14	138
1911	75	2	38	4	78	4	17	218
	402	3	178	8	192	8	84	875

At Chicago

Year	S.C. Buff	R.C. Buff	S.C. Black	R.C. Black	S.C. White	R.C. White	Any other variety	Total
1901	45	..	..	..	..	..	..	45
1902	108	12	..	..	13	..	..	133
1903	88	83	36	..	53	..	34	294
1904	45	15	..	..	35	..	2	97
1905	30	7	8	..	1	12	..	58
1906	37	14	20	..	23	15	6	115
1907	68	12	47	6	11	15	..	159
1910	177	..	48	..	118	8	..	351
	598	143	159	6	254	50	42	1252

Any other variety, as mentioned above, includes the Diamond Jubilee and the Spangled varieties, as well as those that were in an introductory state and therefore had to be exhibited under the class known as "Any other Variety."

It will be noted that the Buffs have been by far the largest class shown at Madison Square, though the Blacks have been a strong class during the last five years. With Rose and Single Comb classes combined there has been 1,077 Buffs, 752 Blacks, 404 Whites and 174 A. O. V. The Buffs have not only led each year, but the exhibit of 1909 was extra large, showing a satisfactory increase in the number of exhibits.

It will be observed that the Orpingtons are not as popular as an exhibition fowl at Boston as they are at New York. The latter place has had on exhibition more than three and one-half times as many Orpingtons since 1901 as has the metropolis of New England. Perhaps one reason for this is: Boston is known as a critical market place for table poultry and eggs. The famous South-Shore products find a ready market in Boston. New Englanders are much in favor of yellow skin and legs and also, prefer dark-shelled or brown eggs. The New York market prefers a white-shelled egg and the presumption is that the New York public takes more kindly to white skinned poultry. Furthermore, we may continue to look for larger classes at Madison Square, as this great show is conceded by exhibitors to be the battle-ground which decides the real championships. This fact alone will continue to attract the larger exhibits to Madison Square Garden. Despite this we believe that market requirements in many sections either add or detract from the number and importance of exhibits.

Although we have not at hand the figures for the 1908 and 1909 Chicago shows, it will be noted that the total for the seven years is larger than the number of Orpingtons exhibited at Boston during the eight years listed. Readers will also notice that the Buffs have a large lead in point of numbers shown at Chicago. Even the Rose Comb Buffs are ahead of any of the other varieties on exhibition at Chicago during the seven years covered by the list.

Summary of the Three American Shows

Total number of S. C. Buffs shown.................1738
Total number of R. C. Buffs shown.................. 231
Total number of S. C. Blacks shown................ 924
Total number of R. C. Blacks shown............... 89
Total number of S. C. Whites shown............... 624
Total number of R. C. Whites shown............... 76
Total number of any other variety.................. 283

Total number of Orpingtons shown 3965

The foregoing table shows that the Buffs lack just twenty-seven birds of equaling in number all the other varieties combined. This showing establishes which is the most popular variety. We are not writing this report to start argument, but with the object of demonstrating the rapid increase in the popularity of the Orpingtons in America, both east and west—a popularity that we believe to be richly deserved. The shows above listed are not only three leading exhibitions, but are representative of a large territory.

The Black and White Orpingtons are gaining rapidly in public favor throughout the country, especially in the west. The Orpingtons today are one of our truly popular breeds and we predict that they will keep on gaining in popularity as an exhibition fowl, because of their utility values which in both England and America have won them a firm position as a general purpose fowl—good for the table and good layers.

BUFF ORPINGTON HEN

Winner of First Prize and Silver Cup, Crystal Palace, England, and numerous First Prizes at American Shows. Owned by Mrs. S. C. Bridgewater, Tennessee.

CHAPTER VIII

What Breeders Say

Orpingtons of the Past, Present and Future — Prominent Breeders Express Their Views on Type and Color — The New Standard Will Help Improve The Breed

O get the views of prominent and successful breeders of Orpingtons, on the progress made in attaining a more uniform type and color in the different varieties, also under the further improvement of the breed under the revised American Standard of Perfection, we sent a list of questions to leading fanciers in the east and west. The contributors to this symposium are:

A. L. Goodwin, Massachusetts.

H. H. Kingston, Jr., New York.

C. A. Moxley, Illinois.

Milton W. Brown, Ohio.

E. A. Haring, Connecticut.

Paul Kyle, New York.

Archibald B. Dalby, New Jersey.

Henrietta E. Hooker, Michigan.

C. S. Byers, Indiana.

C. E. Fisher, Ohio.

E. B. Miller, Indiana.

J. M. Williams, Michigan.

W. H. Gifford, Massachusetts.

Goodes and Palmer, Michigan.

David N. Foster, Indiana.

Henry B. Prescott, New Hampshire.

1. How do Orpingtons of today compare in typical shape, size and color with those bred and exhibited five or more years ago?

"There has been a steady improvement in shape and color in all varieties of Orpingtons in the past five years. As to shape this is especially true of the Buffs and Whites. There is some doubt whether there has been any great advance in the matter of size, with the possible exception of the Blacks."—A. L. Goodwin.

"Taking it for granted that American birds are meant, the Orpington of today is superior in every respect to his forbear of five years ago. showing better type, size and color."—H. H. Kingston, Jr.

"A wonderful improvement."—C. A. Moxley.

"There has been a startling improvement. Winners at big shows five years ago would be worth about $3.00 today. A few individual specimens then approached the present type, but the general average was extremely far from the present ideal."—Milton W. Brown.

"They are much better, especially in shape and color."—E. A. Haring.

"I remember very well the Orpingtons that were exhibited for the first time at the Madison Square Garden,

FIRST & SPECIALS, JAMESTOWN EXPOSITION 1907. OWNED & EXHIBITED BY C. S. BYERS, HAZELRIGG, IND.

which was in 1899. I then noticed the peculiar shape, which indicated to me that the Orpington can grow more meat on her deep long breast than any other fowl. I was so much impressed with that one good point that I bought some and ever since have kept them to my greatest satisfaction. The American fanciers have certainly improved the shape and size of the Orpington hens, compared with those from England exhibited at the Madison Square Garden Show for a number of successive years. The color, particularly in the Buffs, has been improved also, if not changed to a lighter buff than formerly shown. All fanciers, I think, agree to the present shape of the female Orpingtons. In the S. C. Black male classes, however, the American Standard is open for discussion. The Black Orpington male cannot have as long a back as his cousins'. the Buffs or Whites, because one of the ancestors of the Black Orpington was a Black Langshan. Consequently the back of the black male will always be short with broad shoulders. Although a long back has been well established in Black hens, I doubt, however, if fanciers will ever be successful in breeding a long back in the Black Orpington males."—Paul Kyle.

"I think the color has improved but the shape and size have gone back."—Archibald B. Dalby.

"I think the color has improved wonderfully, but have been fearful that this, desirable as it is, would be emphasized at expense of type, and an Orpington is nothing, once the type is lost."—Henrietta E. Hooker.

"In proportion to the number bred by experts there are now many more specimens that approach the present Standard type than there were five or more years ago."—C. S. Byers.

"They compare fairly well, but they seem to have lost in color."—E. B. Miller.

"I saw five years ago what I believe to be as good shaped birds as are found today, but not so many of them. I believe the color has improved more than the shape."—C. E. Fisher.

"Both color and shape have been much improved—especially the former. We are practically away from that Rhode Island Red that bothered so many."—J. M. Williams.

"There is improvement in shape, but not in size and color."—W. H. Gifford.

"Size and color have improved. In some respects the shape has deteriorated. There is too much difference in shape in the different varieties of Orpingtons."—Goodes and Palmer.

"As the market is demanding a different shaped bird now, it is very hard to say how the Orpington of today compares with the Orpington of five years ago. Five years ago the Orpington ran to the Dorking in shape, while now the fancy market demands a broader and deeper bird, more like the larger breeds; also, a shorter shank is sought after, which, to my mind, throws the bird out of proportion. The Standard does not give a short-shanked bird, and in the show room they are not cut much on shank unless the shanks are extremely long."—Col. D. N. Foster.

"They have improved very much during the last five years."—H. B. Prescott.

2. Are the present Standard weights sufficient to bring out the large blocky, or cobby, type demanded by the fanciers of the present day?

"The present Standard weights of the Orpington are entirely sufficient to set off to good advantage the distinctive, blocky type required for the breed. In fact, I believe that the two light colored Orpingtons, the Whites and the Ermines, the latter being the new Orpington with colors of the Light Brahma, both running a trifle lighter in weight than the Blacks, both show this cobby, blocky type to better advantage than any of the other varieties. This is probably due to the very light color of the birds, and would seem to argue that excessive weight is not essential to a handsome Orpington."—A. L. Goodwin.

"The present weights are all the breed can stand, without losing its utility qualities, and are amply sufficient to maintain the present type."—H. H. Kingston, Jr.

"I think so."—C. A. Moxley.

"No. Blacks and Whites could, with advantage, take two more pounds per bird. English breeders have no difficulty in over-topping the Standard weights in Buffs by 50 per cent."—Milton W. Brown.

"I think so, and I think the cobby type is being carried too far. Some of our best awards are going to birds minus their tails."—E. A. Haring.

"The present Standard weights are fully sufficient to bring out the cobby and compact type and shape."—Paul Kyle.

"Most of the birds that are winning prizes are overweight, as called for in the Standard."—Archibald B. Dalby.

"I think they are."—Henrietta E. Hooker.

"Yes."—C. S. Byers.

"I believe the present Standard weights are high enough."—E. B. Miller.

"I think the Standard weights are all right for the present at least."—C. E. Fisher.

"I think so. I have had no trouble with males as to weight, but if I had more weight on females I should have too much fat, which would hurt the laying."—J. M. Williams.

"Cannot see any reason to change weights."—W. H. Gifford.

"We think the present weights are about right. It would perhaps be better if there were higher weights on Buffs, and perhaps Blacks, but if the weights of these varieties are raised, it would be difficult to bring the Whites up to weight."—Goodes and Palmer.

"The Standard weights are to my opinion sufficient to bring out the large blocky type now demanded. The fancier must not lose sight of the utilitarian qualities that all breeds must have if they are to become and stay popular. Get a large fowl, and as a rule the laying qualities of your birds suffer; and when you put them on the market for eating they are too large for most families and the butcher

does not like to handle them—more especially in the cities."—Col. D. N. Foster.

"I find that the Standard weights have to be exceeded to bring out the large blocky birds demanded. Nearly all my customers call for birds over Standard weight."—H. B. Prescott.

3. Do not too many of our modern exhibition specimens show too much fluff, looseness of feathering, and rather too much shortness of legs?

"An Orpington of true type ought not to have to depend upon loose, fluffy feathering to give the desired shape. The Blacks have loose feathers, which fact tends to emphasize the shape. The Whites and Ermines are more closely feathered, and yet as now perfected by the best breeders show the true Orpington type. This shows that loose feathering is not necessary to give the desired type. I have always favored a comparatively short leg for all Orpingtons."—A. L. Goodwin.

"Most emphatically, yes. I have no time for the Orpington that drags its fluff on the ground. Keep the shanks short, out not extreme."—H. H. Kingston, Jr.

"Yes."—C. A. Moxley.

"Yes. Any approach to the Cochin means a distinct deterioration, and extreme shortness of leg seems to go hand in hand with low egg production."—Milton W. Brown.

"I like a bit of fluff, but of course it can be overdone. I think the short leg is being overdone. A large bird requires some length of leg to show it off properly."—E. A. Haring.

BLACK EMPRESS

This Black Orpington hen is owned by Milton W. Brown, proprietor of Cheviot Farms. He writes that she is the dam or granddam of winners at Madison Square Garden, Jamestown Exposition, Boston, Chicago, Cleveland, Allentown and Hagerstown.

"I have not yet noticed too much fluff or looseness of feathers in the Buff or White classes; however, in the Black Orpington classes, particularly the hens, I observe too much fluff and also shortness of legs. An Orpington must be short in legs, but not as low as a Dorking, nor as high as a Plymouth Rock."—Paul Kyle.

"Yes."—Archibald B. Dalby.

"I know many have this feeling, but I have not wished to get too far from the Cochin type—then we have a Buff Rock, minus color of legs."—Henrietta E. Hooker.

"No."—C. S. Byers.

"I have always thought so, and have therefore bred closer feathers and longer legs. The birds seem to forage better and lay better, and mine are farm-raised and bred for profit and utility."—E. B. Miller.

"I do not believe in the 'high' Orpington, and I like a good fluff. To my eye a medium low Orpington, with good fluff to round out shape, makes a very beautiful bird."—C. E. Fisher.

"I do not like too much fluff, and find that those of my birds which are closely feathered are more profitable as a commercial bird than the loose-feathered fowl. I am not in favor of encouraging the shortness of the legs. If feathers are not quite so fluffy, they will not look so short-legged."—J. M. Williams.

"There is not too much fluff, and when you lengthen the legs and take away the loose feathering, you will bring the Orpington to a type more like the Langshan. Some talk of changes in shape, and that will throw the birds nearer the Rocks in type."—W. H. Gifford.

"There is a tendency to get the Orpingtons with the loose fluffy feathers, while the Standard calls for a tightly-feathered bird. I like to see them with the fluffy feathers, although I have always tried to keep the Duke of Kent strain of Black Orpingtons to the tight feather, as the Standard calls for this."—David N. Foster.

"Many specimens show too much fluff, but I seldom see them too short in legs. In general, I see too many long in legs—which is especially true of the Whites."—Goodes and Palmer.

"I think some breeders have carried the shortness of legs a bit farther than the best good of the breed demands."—H. B. Prescott.

4. Do you think the revised American Standard of Perfection, in placing more value on the shape and less on the color of Orpingtons, will prove of material benefit in obtaining more uniform type in exhibition specimens?

Second Cockerel, Chicago, 1909. Bred and raised by Goodes & Palmer, Marcellus, Mich.

"It should have been comprehended a long time ago by the rank and file of Orpington breeders that the utmost value should be placed on shape and type, and the question of color made a secondary consideration. A few of the leading Orpington breeders were big enough to realize this, and the day was saved for the Orpington. All breeders who do any exhibiting at all must necessarily see the necessity of keeping to the type, sooner or later. This, and the position of the revised Standard of Perfection, will aid materially in establishing uniformity of type."—A. L. Goodwin.

"I have always championed type in Orpingtons in preference to color. Get type first, then go after color. I think the revision referred to above is a step in the right direction."—H. H. Kingston, Jr.

"Yes—and no. Yes, as to exhibition qualities; no, as to shape, which is wrong now. The Standard shape, in my judgment, is detrimental to the utilitarian qualities of this breed. I prefer a little more length of body and legs, for best results."—C. A. Moxley.

"Decidedly, where judging is critical. After all, it will always remain to some extent a matter of view point of the individual judge."—Milton W. Brown.

"I think shape and color go hand in hand, and I value one about as much as the other—at least, I put color a very close second. It is no easy trick to breed good colored Orpingtons, and it is hard to value good color too highly if combined with Orpington type. Once lost, it is not easily gotten again."—E. A. Haring.

"I believe the revised American Standard of Perfection should place more value on the shape of the Orpingtons and less on color. It is the peculiar Orpington shape which makes an exact and gratifying distinction."—Paul Kyle.

"Yes."—Archibald B. Dalby.

"I think both should be kept in sight, but the Standard may help."—Henrietta E. Hooker.

"Yes."—C. S. Byers.

"I believe many breeders have lost ground on shape of birds in their attempts to improve the color, and I think they would do well to breed for shape and size, and let color go—that is, for the next five years; for I believe they will not lose much in color and will gain much in shape and size."—E. B. Miller.

"The revised American Standard of Perfection, in placing more value on shape than on color, will, probably bring better shaped birds to the show room; but I am wondering if it will not be at the sacrifice of color. I have seen better shaped Orpingtons, in my opinion, the past year, than I have colored ones. The Buff color is not what I should like it to be, and if we are to drop color and breed for shape, I think it is surely a serious mistake."—C. E. Fisher.

"Yes, by all means."—J. M. Williams.

"I think we should put all the value we can on shape, and no less on color. Some specimens exhibited last winter were small because of late hatches, but having been housed early, they had better color. If we are going to have Orpingtons, let's have them low and cobby, and unlike Rocks and Langshans."—W. H. Gifford.

"We should think it would help. The color gives us less trouble than shape."—Goodes and Palmer.

"I think it would be of greater benefit if more stress were laid on shape than on color, as every one knows what the color should be, while hardly any two judges have the same type in mind when they are judging; and the same is true with the different breeders. This is the reason that a bird will score differently under different judges. These things should be made very plain in the Standard and judges should conform to the Standard, regardless of what their opinion is as to how an Orpington should look."—D. N. Foster.

"I do. I consider shape of the first importance."—H. B. Prescott.

S·C·W·ORPINGTON C·K·R·L. HEADING ONE OF THE BREEDING YARDS AT RIDGE VIEW FARMS WILLOUGHBY OHIO.

CHAPTER IX

Orpingtons As Utility Fowl

Relative Value of the Three Standard Varieties as Layers and Meat Producers Carefully and Clearly Presented

Edward Brown, F. L. S., England

Editor's Note:—The following excellent article, giving the relative merits of the Black, White and Buff Orpingtons as utility fowls, was written by Professor Brown, who has devoted many years to the study of the practical qualities of all domesticated races of poultry and which appeared in "The Illustrated Poultry Record," December, 1908.

POPULARITY is a fickle jade, with hens as with humans. The fact of a race of poultry attaining a large measure of public favor for a time is no proof of its virtues. Breeds rise and fall in general estimation without any apparent reason. Some are boomed into prominence, ascending with meteoric brilliancy, and, after a shower of pyrotechnics, disappear, coming down like the proverbial stick. Others have to fight for their recognition at first, and only succeed when they have proved their merits. Yet more are slow in winning a place, but hold it for a considerable period when secured, ultimately descending into semi-oblivion with slow and graceful steps. A few appear to withstand both prosperity and adversity, reasserting themselves again and yet again. All, however, serve a purpose—if we can but recognize it—contributing their share to the progression of the poultry industry. The final court of appeal with respect to any breed is not its beauty or its coloration, but the practical nature of its qualities. Otherwise the popularity attained is limited or evanescent.

Many, nay most, breeds have suffered more from their supporters than their critics. "Save me from my friends" may be the cry of all grades. Some years ago, when writing to an American friend, I said that "if we believed everything claimed for the Orpington we should expect to find it the only breed on the Plains of Heaven—if fowls are to be found there." This was not stated with any desire to minimize the economic qualities of the race, which are great, but to show that exaggeration is met with even where it is least needed. And certainly no breed has required such exuberant advocacy less than the one under review. Its sterling merits have been widely recognized, more in one variety than in others. They speak for themselves, which is ever the best form of advertisement. Idealism is necessary, we suppose for progress. We like to hug our vain conceits. But when those who are less blinded by personal predilection or interest humbly venture to point out that there may be weaknesses which we had omitted to notice, surely these gentle souls should not be regarded and attacked as if they were minions of the Evil One. I can say this with respect to the Orpington, a race for which so much that is favorable can be stated, in the hope that even if the conclusions arrived at may not be entirely and completely favorable, I may receive a measure of absolution.

For the purpose of the present review it will be necessary to confine our attention to three varieties, namely, the Black, the Buff, and the White. The others, whose number I am frankly uncertain about, are at present purely exhibition stock and have yet to prove their economic value. However, much fanciers may wish to multiply varieties, utility poultry breeders are well advised to abstain from speculations of that kind. Hence I do not propose to burden these remarks with details of no real value. "Handsome is as handsome does," and we are specially interested in the "does" side of things. If the exhibitor will kindly improve these sub-varieties on practical lines we shall be glad; but we want to know as soon as he has done so, and before he has had time to ruin them by undue exaltation of arbitrary and useless points. Probably they may never be of any real service, in which case we are content to leave them to him entirely until the crack of doom.

Taking the last three of the varieties named first, by reason of the fact that there is least to be said respecting it, as it has yet to prove its value fully, up to the present it has not been adopted widely. A few breeders have introduced it, but hitherto it has been mainly in the hands of specialist breeders or exhibitors. Last year, when in Denmark, I was interested to find that at a breeding center in that country the White Orpington was exclusively kept and was being distributed with the object of securing tinted shelled eggs and improving winter laying, both of which had been achieved. On that side it is more than probable that the White Orpington will prove of great service, although it has fairly good table properties. Like the Blacks, it is heavier in bone than the Buffs, and consequently takes longer in attainment of a killing condition, whilst the structure of body indicates more thigh development than is desirable in a first-class table fowl. Hence, in spite of its white legs, flesh, and skin, the Danes appear to be right in regarding the flesh qualities of this variety as of less importance than its productiveness as a layer.

For the spring chicken trade it is less serviceable than as a well grown winter fowl. At the Danish breeding center of Sejling, as recorded in my "Report on the Poultry Industry in Denmark and Sweden" a flock of White Orpington hens averaged 74 eggs from November 1, 1906, to March 3, 1907, that is in four months. There was considerable variation in the laying, varying from 93 to 210 in the twelve months. But, the report states, "out of 46 hens trap-nested, five produced less than 120 eggs and nine less than 130, so that the average was good." The eggs are excellent in size and nicely, though not deeply, tinted. My own judgment is that the breeders will be well advised to pay special attention to the development of egg production in this variety, even though the flesh properties are sacrificed to some extent, rather than attempt to run both together, as I do not anticipate that it will ever be of much service as a table breed. It is the direction named that the greater profit will be obtained.

The first of the Orpington family was the Black, introduced twenty-two years ago, the popularity of which grew very rapidly indeed. There can be no question that they met admirably a need arising from the great extension about that period of poultry-keeping in suburban and manufacturing districts, where a dark plumaged fowl is almost a necessity, and where a bird of quiet disposition, willing to submit itself to a restricted environment, yet vigorous and economically profitable, is sure to command a large amount of favor. For such conditions the general purpose type fowl was more suitable than the non-sitters. Some of the older races of this class were losing vigor, and the Black Orpingtons "filled the bill." It is a large fowl, hardy, a good winter layer, but not very prolific, the eggs having a moderate tint of shell. It is somewhat heavy in bone and, therefore, rather slow in growth, but this, if not an actual recommendation, was no disadvantage under the conditions named, and to many poultry keepers the uniformity of color was a decided gain. It has been claimed that this variety is a first-class table fowl, but that cannot be conceded. That it is fairly good may be freely acknowledged. The meat is too much upon the thighs to take the highest place, and as it is grey rather than white in flesh and skin, it can never hope to attain the supreme rank. The flesh is abundant, however, and well flavored. Signs are evident that the Black Orpington has largely accomplished its purpose, and under suburban and other like conditions, where all-round qualities are desired, it may be safely recommended.

Probably the most popular variety of fowl is the Buff Orpington, in spite of the fact that it does not equal the White Leghorn or the White Wyandotte as an egg producer, or the Sussex, the Bresse, or the Dorking for its table properties. Nor is it on the exhibition side that its reputation is wholly built, though in that respect it occupies a leading position in this country. What, then, may be asked, is the explanation? To which we may answer that it is the combination of qualities and its adaptability that account for the unique position held by the variety. The fact cannot be gainsaid that at home and abroad it has deservedly won the place now occupied by it. Throughout the United Kingdom practical poultry keepers have adopted it to a very large extent. During my visits to Hungary in 1902 and 1904 I found that it was extensively bred, and that the agricultural authorities in that country were advocating its dissemination as the breed specially suitable to meet the growing trade for eggs and chickens. Two years ago I found it had been received with marked favor in Canada and it is making its way slowly but steadily, in the United States. The same was seen to be the case in Sweden last year, and this season hundreds of Buff Orpingtons have been distributed in the Province of Scane by the Agricultural Society in that country. We know, also, that large numbers have been exported to the colonies and foreign countries. The secret is found in the combination of tinted shelled eggs met with in very few races. It is a fairly good layer, especially in winter, and is certainly good in meat qualities, whilst its quiet temperament makes it easily restrained. Moreover the considerable infusion of yellow blood which it embodies enables it to be kept upon heavy soils where other white-

fleshed races would not thrive, even though the lighter soils are more favorable for obtaining the best results.

One great advantage which the Buff Orpington possesses over other members of the same family is in the distribution of the flesh found thereon. Light in bone, it does not carry so much muscle upon the thighs and the flesh is exceedingly well developed on the sternum, whilst that flesh is white and cobby. In length of body it cannot

AN ENGLISH WINNING ORPINGTON.

Above is shown one of the winning birds bred by Miss S. Carey, Toynton Rectory, Spilsby, England. He was winner of Victoria Memorial Challenge Trophy and Ladies' Challenge Cup, besides many other firsts.

equal some other breeds, but the plump and well-filled skin gives it a pleasing appearance. We have not found this breed a rapid grower, in which respect, however, it is better than many of the heavy breeds. The eggs are a little small, and here improvement ought to be secured. I am convinced, however, that breeders should pay most attention to the table qualities of the Buffs, and by striving to maintain lightness of bone, to keep the wings large, and thus tend to improve the breast qualities, retain and extend the qualities which have made it popular. Plumage coloration is of very secondary importance.

Orpingtons in International Egg Laying Contests

D. E. Hale

THE following contests that are generally spoken of as the Australian contests, have demonstrated some interesting facts, and one is, that the Orpingtons are a great all-around fowl, a fine winter layer and one of the most profitable breeds that have been entered in the contests.

The second annual contest which was held at Hawkesbury Agricultural College, N. S. Wales, 1903-04, was won by a pen of S. L. Wyandottes with an average of 218 eggs each.

Black Orpingtons were second, with an average of 212 1-3 eggs each. There were 14 pens of Black Orpingtons entered, which laid 14,118 eggs, or an average of 168 3-42 eggs per fowl.

The third annual contest held 1904-05, at the same place, was again won by the S. L. Wyandottes, while the Black Orpingtons stood fifth.

The Wyandottes laid 1224 eggs or, an average of 204 eggs each. The Orpingtons laid 1155 eggs or an average of 192½ eggs each.

There were 18 pens of Black Orpingtons entered, which laid 17,224 eggs, or an average of 158 13-17 eggs each.

There were 10 pens of Buff Orpingtons, which laid 8677 eggs, or an average of 144 37-60 eggs each.

For the three months winter test, the Black Orpingtons stood third and were also third, for the market value of eggs for the 12 months.

The reports show that the weather throughout the rainy season was exceptionally bad, keeping the ground soaked most of the time, causing very damp, chilly, disagreeable conditions.

BLACK ORPINGTONS, ENTERED BY MR. W. WILD, LAKE ALBERT.

Winners of Second Prize for greatest number (1,274) of eggs laid during the twelve months at the Second International Twelve Months' Laying Competition, Hawkesbury Agricultural College, April, 1903-March, 1904. Eighth Prize for first six months (winter); and Fifth Prize for market value.

Australian Egg-laying Contest

The year before, two parts corn, to one part wheat was fed, among other feeds, and during this third contest, there was two parts wheat to one part corn fed, thereby demonstrating that corn is a better food for egg production, than it has been given credit.

The fourth annual contest was held at the same place, 1905-06, the Single Comb White Leghorns winning first prize, with an average of 235 1-6 eggs each, a grand record for that time. The Black Orpingtons won eighth place in

TYPICAL LAYING HEN
One of the Australian Egg-laying Contest Black Orpington winners that averaged 177 eggs per hen during the 1908-09 contest. A typical hen from Mr. Wild's pen.

this contest, the winning pen laying 1188 eggs, or an average of 196 eggs each.

There were 19 pens of Black Orpingtons, that laid 18,011 eggs, or an average of 157 113-114 eggs each; a pretty fair average for 114 fowls.

There were 5 pens of Buff Orpingtons entered, that laid 4,727 eggs, or an average of 157 17-30 eggs each.

The general utility prize, open to hens averaging at least 6 pounds in weight and laying eggs averaging not less than 24 ounces per dozen, was won by the Black Orpingtons.

While it was a grand honor to win the laying contest, it is also a great honor to win the general utility prize, for it is the general utility fowl that is in demand today.

The reports of the fifth annual contest held 1906-07, and the sixth annual contest held 1907-08, we have been unable to get.

The seventh annual contest for 1908-09 ended as follows: White Leghorns laid the most eggs, namely, 1,379, or an average of 229 5-6 eggs each. The S. C. Black Orpingtons were second with 1,288 eggs or an average of 214-2-3 eggs each.

There were eleven pens of Black Orpingtons entered in the contest and four pens of White Orpingtons. The average number of eggs laid by the Blacks were a fraction over 177 eggs per hen. The Whites averaged a fraction over 115 eggs each.

The highest number of eggs laid in one month was laid by a pen of Black Orpingtons, 159 eggs, or an average of 26½ eggs per hen, a wonderful record for one month. The Black Orpingtons made the largest net profit per hen as they laid the best, when eggs were high.

Buff Orpingtons Ideal Market Fowl

W. B. Borders

IPREFER the S. C. Buff variety on account of their beautiful plumage and for the further reason that I live in the city, and believe that they will stand close confinement and not show the dirt as much as the other varieties. I find that they will be fully feathered at the age of six to eight weeks and that they will weigh two pounds by the time they are fully feathered.

They will begin laying at the age of about five months, if forced, but as the forcing is liable to ruin them as two-year old breeders, I try to lengthen the time to five and a half to six months. By doing this you are also able to grow larger birds and the progeny will be the better for the delay.

The hatching of show birds depends on the manner of handling them before the shows. I make it a practice to hatch during each month from January to July 1st, but find that the birds hatched in May and June will make the best showing, if large enough, and there is no doubt but that they will be up to Standard weight if given proper care and food.

I use trap nests in all my breeding pens and keep a record of the number of eggs laid by each female during the breeding season, but have never kept them for the whole year, so cannot give yearly records. I have but one female that laid 117 eggs in 126 days and a pen of six pullets that averaged 108 eggs in the same time. In mating my pens I use only progeny from my best layers and by doing this year to year, hope to improve the whole flock.

I have always found a ready sale for all the birds I could raise. In fact last year I did not have a bird to sell after the first of March. The demand for high-class birds is on the increase in the west and the western breeders are being educated to buy the best as they find it pays in the end. The price does not seem to matter so long as the best of quality is furnished.

The color of the skin and legs seem to increase the demand in the local market as they present a cleaner appearance when dressed. If the Orpington Standard was to be changed to read yellow legs and skin, I feel that the popularity of the breed would decrease to such an extend that they would be dropped in a few years. In fact it would be hard to tell them from the Buff Rocks, as a great many breeders do not seem to be able to tell the difference in shape, if you take their birds as an example of their judgment.

If I were to make an ideal all around fowl it would be the same as the S. C. Buff Orpington is today, as I believe they come as near filling the wants of the fancier and general breeder as any variety we have in the Standard. They will lay in the most severe winter weather when eggs are high in price as well as late in the fall when other varieties are resting.

The chicks will grow more ounces in a given time than almost any other kind of chickens. They are very hardy and are not as susceptible to diseases as are some of the other varieties. In fact the Orpingtons are the only bird as far as I am concerned.

A partial bird's-eye view showing houses and yards at Hawkesbury Agricultural College, New South Wales, where are held the well-known Australian Egg-laying Contests.

CHAPTER X

Conditioning and Training Fowls for Exhibition

Training and Posing Necessary. What to Feed. Milk as a Conditioner. Importance of Dry Sound Grains, Animal and Vegetable Foods. Health, Vigor and Stamina Essential to Success

J. H. Drevenstedt

THE fact of a bird being well fed and groomed, showing splendid condition, while absolutely necessary and essential in competing for the prizes at our modern poultry shows, is not always sufficient in a tight place where two specimens are about equal in merit and in condition. This is where proper training of the show specimens will often determine the result. We remember an instance of this kind which occurred at the Madison Square Garden ten or more years ago. It was in the palmy days of the Buff Cochins when such noted fanciers as the Sharp Bros. of Taunton, Mass., and Adams, Purdue, and Young of Orange, N. J., made great entries of the once famed Buffs. The pick of English and American flocks could be seen at the Garden in those days. The manager for Messrs. Sharp was an experienced conditioner and had his charges in beautiful fettle. Their plumage glistened and every little detail was looked after so that no fault could be found with grooming.

George Purdue, a past master in the art of feeding and conditioning birds, had his birds in equally fine condition as those in charge of Mr. Marshall. Bue he went just a little beyond that, he had his birds trained to the hour. No sooner was one of these birds touched by the judge's stick, than it would seem to know what was wanted and the proper pose was seldom lacking. One huge scholar especially was an apt scholar and would stand and look his prettiest when handled by the judge. And that pose won the blue ribbon.

Edward B. Thompson, of Barred Plymouth Rock Ringlet fame, is another great believer in training his show birds. At a show held in Troy, N. Y., in the early nineties the creator of the famous Ringlet Rocks exhibited a cockerel that "did stunts," to use Mr. Thompson's expression. In other words the bird was a great pet and was taught to jump over rods and through the arms of his owner, remain in a statuesque pose when stroked under the lower mandible or touched with the judging stock. It is needless to say that this bird attracted much attention, especially from the judge who simply could not resist the temptation to put the blue ribbon on its cage. The famous old Plymouth Rock hen, "Helen of Troy" was another one of Mr. Thompson's trained troupe of performing chickens. The cockerel he exhibited at Madison Square Garden and won the blue ribbon with, was most carefully trained and a splendid actor in the show pen. It is not going "behind the returns" to say that this training was largely responsible for the award going to the cockerel, for there were several other cockerels there that some breeders preferred to the winner, but they lacked that finishing touch without which the chances in a hot class at a Madison Square Garden Show, are greatly reduced.

A bird that has not been retarded in its growth from the time it was hatched until nearly feathered out, is easily conditioned for the show. There is nothing better than sound red wheat and Canadian flint corn to put it in condition when the birds are at liberty and have a good pasture to forage over. When finished indoors, more care must be taken in using the proper grains. A mixture of cracked corn and crushed oats in equal parts makes the best dry mash with red wheat for a whole grain. Granulated beef scraps of the best sterilized brand, given in small quantity twice a week will furnish the cheapest and best animal food. Vegetable food ise best supplied by either mangel wurzels, cabbage or lettuce leaves. But there is just one food that is superior to all others in bringing birds up to a high condition and that is milk.

Milk as a Conditioner.

An English breeder in a recent issue of *Poultry* speaks of the value of milk as follows: "Nowadays condition plays such an important part in the successful exhibiting of a bird that only two or three weeks special feeding will ensure its being put down in first rate form. Personally, I think the finest 'conditioner' there is, and the finest 'conditioner' that could be desired is milk and from what I have seen among big Rock and Wyandotte exhibitors in the North and elsewhere, I should say this opinion is shared by a good many. The extraordinary value of it in this direction is, I believe, known to but few amateurs; at any rate, very few take advantage of it in any useful way. To be really efficacious, it must play a part in almost everything the fowl eats or drinks for at least a fortnight. The drinking troughs must be filled with it twice a day, and the mashes likewise must be

WINNER OF FIRST, NEW YORK DEC 27, 1909-JAN 1, 1910
OWNED BY H. H. KINGSTON JR. ROCHESTER N.Y.

BUFF ORPINGTON COCK

greater force to the large prototype, the Exhibition Game. The decadence of the latter as a popular show fowl has been a source of regret to many old line fanciers, who bred this aristocrat of featherdom for pure love of the Game fowl."

Exhibition Games cannot be raised in close quarters and without proper care and environments. They can be raised in the mountains of New York and New England, if allowed the freedom of range their nature demands, and their constitution is dependent on. To obtain the hard feather, the muscle and bone that make the Game fowl the athlete of all fowl, requires open air culture and the simple life. This means hardiness and splendid physical condition, which no artificial methods have been able to supplant. In fact, if you wish to raise superior Games and Game Bantams, the latter may not be the only way, but it certainly is the easiest way.

This reminds us of a little experience we had in 1888, the year the Newburg, N. Y. show was held. We had a pen of Golden Spangled Hamburgs on exhibition, which by their fine condition attracted the attention of Sherman Hartwell, a veteran breeder of Partridge Cochins from the Nutmeg State. Mr. Hartwell asked us how we got these birds in such fine shape and we informed him that they were farm raised, well fed and had never been indoors since they were old enough to roost in the trees of an apple orchard, and we picked out the pen by lantern light from the flock that roosted in an open shed after they had been taken from the trees in November. "Well," remarked Deacon Hartwell, "that's about the way I condition my Partridge Cochins, but of course they can't fly high enough to roost in trees, so they take to the nearest fence."

It is needless to say that while such methods were productive of good results 20 or more years ago, they would not do in this age, when every bird must be prepared weeks before a show to get a place in the awards. The principle was correct as far as health, vigor and stamina was concerned, but the finishing touches had to be put on under cover where rain and sun could not affect the new plumage. The latter is especially important in the preparation of buff fowl for the show. To produce a buff bird in "silk attire" requires very careful handling. Successful breeders of buff varieties of poultry are very careful in providing the proper quarters for their growing young stock and the moulting old ones, especially in the fall of the year when the new feathers begin to push forth from the old ones. Shade from the sun and shelter from the rain are the two important factors in the ultimate success of producing rich golden buff plumage. One very successful breeder of Buff Cochin Bantams keeps his young and old stock under cover from the time the new plumage starts until it is fully grown. Breeding Cochin Bantams, he naturally keeps them in a small area, to retard any growth toward legginess and to increase the length and retain any volume of the foot feathering. The same rule will apply to Buff, White, Black and Partridge Cochins.

With Brahmas we believe Old Dame Nature is the best "conditioner." Give the Light Brahma the range, the exercise, and the same sound grain, breeders of Plymouth Rocks, Wyandottes and Rhode Island Reds give their fowls, and you will have Brahmas that are correct in type and second to none in egg production and market properties. The Brahma is not a Cochin, consequently does not require a restricted range and close confinement to grow a huge bunch of feathers on body, fluff and legs and toes. Like the American varieties, they will require

mixed entirely with it. Given this continually, the birds that are intended for show will quickly come to hand and be in prime condition when they are wanted. The other items of dietary should be quite as usual. Special dieting and extra feeding are quite unnecessary and indeed undesirable because show fowls thrive far better when treated like ordinary beings, and it is my experience that the more one fusses about one's best birds, the worse they fare and the less keen become their appetites. They must be kept clean, however, and everything around them must be clean and neat. Time spent attending to these matters is time well spent. Vessels in which milk has been placed require special attention as milk is apt to coagulate in the bottom, the effects of which are far from salutary."

The above advice is sound and, if followed, good results are bound to follow. Milk is not fed as extensively to chickens in the United States as in England and Canada except in a few localities near Philadelphia and Washington where milk fed chickens for market are largely and profitably produced. But there are a few fanciers who fully realize the great value of milk, and one in particular, George W. Mitchell, uses a liberal supply to grow his famous Partridge Cochins, while his manager, Adolph Anderson, has produced the largest and finest White Cochins in the country by using the milk diet liberally. Mr. McNeil of Canada is another believer in milk as food, and where length of feather is desired, the lacteal fluid is superior to all other foods. Years ago, when engaged in dairy farming, we used considerable milk for the young chickens giving it to them from the start, but we diluted it with one half boiling water, which we found kept the milk in better condition in warm weather.

Grain Foods

There are prepared grain foods on the market that are excellent for conditioning fowls in confinement, but our advice to the purchasers is: Be sure to buy the best regardless of the price. Grain is high, that is sound sweet wheat, barley, oats or corn, and no such thing as a "cheap ration" should be considered.

As to Games and Game Bantams, we will say that the best way to condition such birds is to provide unlimited range, in the woods if possible, feed them a ground oats, barley and dry bran mash, using one-third by weight of each, with sound wheat and Canadian flint corn as a scratching food.

Dan Clayton, the most successful breeder of Brown Red Game Bantams in England is a great believer in the value of Canadian corn as a food for his Bantams. His birds are raised in movable coops on grassy plots and have unlimited range. The corn seems to put them in prime condition, bringing out the luster of the plumage in a remarkable degree.

Pigeon fanciers are well aware of the value of this yellow corn, and chicken fanciers would be if they realized its value as a conditioning food. The high price, however, has acted as a barrier to its more extensive use. Canadian flint corn is the small variety of maize known in the United States as Dutton corn. It is a very hard grain when old, and the harder the grain, the better the result will be. It keeps the chickens busy grinding it, and this has a beneficial influence on the health of the birds. Birds fed and reared in such a way need no condition powders to stimulate their appetites or improve their condition. Although the above comments were written with the Game Bantam in view, they will apply with even very little conditioning prior to a show, if they have had a bountiful supply of ozone and range on grassy lawns or pastures.

Natural Conditioning

Some of the best conditioned White Leghorns we ever saw were raised in Western New York. They were hatched in incubators and placed in brooders, the latter being set along the edges of a growing field of corn; as the corn grew up the little Leghorns had the time of their lives scratching in the rows and getting the warm May and June sun. When the stalks of corn towered way above their heads in the broiling sun of July and August the rapidly maturing Leghorns enjoyed the grateful shade and grew into handsome, vigorous specimens that were pure white in plumage and sporting rich yellow legs and beaks. They needed no further conditioning except to clean the legs and rub the combs with a little vaseline; the plumage would shine if rubbed with a silk handkerchief. Later in the fall the birds were housed, of course, and those selected for exhibition were placed in roomy pens, the floors of which were covered with straw or shavings and kept scrupulously clean. They won about as many prizes in strong competition as modern birds, specially prepared and washed do in these days.

Assuming that birds have been properly conditioned and trained, we come to the final preparation for the showroom and that is grooming the plumage, the combs and the legs.

Washing White Birds

The following method of washing white fowl is employed by one of the largest exhibitors in the country:

"Having selected or purchased the birds you intend to show, it behooves you to have your birds, when placed before the critical eye of the judge, appear in the best condition possible. About ten days before the show select your birds and place them singly, or if to be shown in pens, place your four pen females together, to prevent fighting when you put them in the exhibition coop, in a room or large coop. If you have no regulation exhibition coops it will pay you to buy two or three. Bed the coops with cut straw, if possible, or coarse shavings. Feed the birds a variety of grain with some green food. Keep grit before them all the time as well as fresh water. Handle the birds all you can, being careful not to break a wing feather, for remember your Standard says cut one-half point for every broken wing feather. Take your latest illustrated Standard, if you have one, and if not buy one, for you cannot select exhibition birds without a Standard.

"If you have a small number to exhibit, prepare to wash your birds four days before the show. First, clean up your coops nicely, putting in fresh straw, and see to it that there is no dust on side of coop, on wires or in the room. If possible, have a warm place to wash your birds. Heat a boiler of soft water and secure four washing tubs. In the first tub place four inches of luke-warm water, just warm enough to cut dirt nicely. In tubs two and three place five or six inches of luke-warm water. Have tub four nearly full of water, with chill off. This tub is to be used for the bluing water. Make bluing water a little stronger in blue than if bluing white clothes. Take a cake of Ivory soap, a soft sponge, several Turkish towels and a couple of palm-leaf fans and you are ready.

"Place bird in tub number one, thoroughly wetting the feathers in every section of the plumage. Keep left hand on back of bird, so it cannot fly out of tub. Always rub with the plumage, never against it. After you have the bird wet, use soap, beginning at head and hackle, washing clean; then the back, tail, fluff, breast and body in rotation as named. After you have washed the bird clean, get all the water you can out of plumage and then place bird in tub number two. Thoroughly rinse bird, taking a sponge and getting clean water through every part of plumage, using one hand to loosen the feathers. Take plenty of time for this and when you have all soap washed out, place bird in tub number three and do the work over again. In this way you are sure to get all soap out of the plumage.

"Washing birds is not such a difficult job once you get the knack. After getting all water possible out of plumage, dip bird in bluing water, letting it drain, and then get all water possible out of plumage again. Now place bird on a barrel covered with clean cloth so there is no danger of the bird getting dirty; take sponge and get all water possible out of plumage, with the towel dry plumage as much as possible, then take fans and fan bird, all the time picking out the plumage, that is separating the feathers. This will make bird fluffy and fine when dried. Place bird in a warm room or near a warm stove, not too close to a hot stove, for the heat will curl the damp feathers, and ruin your work. In a few hours the bird will be dry and as white as snow.

"The bird is thoroughly dry, now you must clean its legs, every scale must be cleaned the same as you would under your finger nails, toes and all. Then rub with sweet oil and alcohol, half and half, to brighten and smooth off the knife scratches.

"For head and face, just cleanse while in the show room with witch hazel, or the sweet oil mixture; not too much or too often with the witch hazel, as it will cause a white scale to form all over the head. If you have done your work well, your bird is at his best and ready for the judge and you have, in a perfectly legitimate way, put from two to five points on him."

In looking over Barred Plymouth Rocks, or any other parti-colored variety, it is necessary to examine every section and remove the old or dead feathers. This is perfectly legitimate and does not constitute what some would call "faking." It is also a well known fact that Barred Plymouth Rocks need just a little more plucking than simply removing the old or dead feathers. An occasional black feather needs to be removed or perhaps a poorly placed or poorly barred one. In Silver Wyandotte females the backs may need looking after. Overlapping feathers sometimes destroy the harmony of the lacing. The same applies to other laced varieties of fowl.

If every breeder who exhibits his birds at poultry shows will be as careful in getting them fit, as he or she is careful to appear in the best "bib and tucker" at a social or church gathering, there would be less fault found with condition birds in the showroom, and much more satisfaction gained by winning prizes on birds because they were "fit as fiddles." Every legitimate means should be employed to win a prize, but "faking," as defined in the American Standard of Perfection is made unlawful by the Association rules and should not be practiced.

Made in the USA
Las Vegas, NV
27 April 2023

71056627R00048